LIVING WITH
MERLIN

LIVING WITH MERLIN

Coping with grief, living life

ANITA BAKSHI

PARTRIDGE
A Penguin Random House Company

To order additional copies of this book, contact
Partridge India
000 800 10062 62
orders.india@partridgepublishing.com

www.partridgepublishing.com/india

CONTENTS

DEDICATION

To my sweetheart

LIFE IS OVER

"For I have touched the lowest point of my existence,
The immeasurable depths of despair"

I can't believe it. It's not true, not possible. It can't be. How is it possible that he's gone? I still cannot use the word dead without an icy feeling of dread engulfing my very soul, a feeling of overwhelming horror at its sheer finality. They lie to me, all these people around me, my family, my friends and the many so-called well-wishers.

"He's gone to a better place. He will not be in pain and he won't suffer there".

This is Aunt Leela, a well meaning, gentle, placid lady in her seventies who hasn't seen any grief closer than losing her nearly 100 year old mother the previous year. To her death is a natural event and a part of our lives and must be accepted as such. She goes on

"I know how you must feel but life must go on . . ."

Dad, my father, is there by my side, as he has been through this whole nightmarish chain of events, from the start, the illness, the treatment, everything. My strength during all the pain and suffering he is here today to give me support, hold me up. He grieves with me and my pain is his too and as I watch him, tired and somehow broken by this tragedy, I wonder again why God wrote this in his larger plan.

"I know how you must feel but life goes on"

How sick I am of hearing this phrase, it's a kind of hello that people use when they don't really know what to say, a kind of start to a conversation. Or a string that is meant for someone to pick up and carry on in an equally meaningless fashion for an absolutely futile attempt at consolation, an uncomforting set of phrases that are mouthed in a kind of parody for providing some solace in grief.

She knows how I feel, oh does she?
And how does she know?

And what about that bit that one about him having gone to a better place. That is completely unacceptable.

A better place? A place where he can be happy without me?

Without me??

That is not possible. He, who wouldn't even be able to take his meals on time if I went to a conference for 2 days, will be happy in a place where I'm not there?

What are all these people trying to tell me?

They're all crazy and don't know what they are talking about. I shut my mind to all of them and think to myself

It's all a bad dream, a nightmare. Any minute now the doorbell will ring and Diven will be standing there, in that all too familiar fashion, with one hand holding the leather strap of that bag he loves to carry all his stuff in and the other hand resting on the side of the wall. The slight slouch and his head thrown a little back so that his hair doesn't fall on his face. And he'll be home again.

For days on end, even months I was like this, unable to really accept what was staring at me in the face and going on day in and day out like a zombie and expecting it to suddenly end and my life return to being my life again. Because, this wasn't my life. How could it be?

My life is a life with Diven all around it. I wake up to him or rather he wakes me up and then goes around starting a clangor of noises designed to ensure that even the dead can't sleep. Puts on the television, that's called a subcortical reflex action where the male of the species is concerned, then takes off to the loo where he invariably drops the ashtray or something. And then, leaving every light burning, he goes to the kitchen.

By this time all this movement has woken me up and I snuggle down, waiting, as I invariably and happily have done for years, for him to give me that first cup of tea in the morning that turns me into a waking human being. Ok so that's how we begin our day, which is normally a dull, boring and mundane day. After my tea, which is around 6 am, I start to get dressed to go for my morning walk. Fancy track pants, branded keds and a sports bra. Pulling all this on and then topping it off with a nice T-shirt and a woolen scarf it its chilly.

While getting dressed I give half an ear to the daily dose of advice I get from my husband

"Don't go too far, stay in the colony. There's no shortage of crazies. You keep hearing all kinds of things"

No shortage of crazies I often think. No definitely not.

"Stay away from the main road. It's early and the trucks are often speeding. Its at these times you get the maximum hit and run accidents, you know"

As I finish dressing I take a look at myself in the mirror and apply a touch of lipstick. And am told

"What's the lipstick for? Who is going to see you at this time?"

"Just like that, I like to. You never know"

Back from my walk, a quick bath and then breakfast and I go off to work after having often being told as I am dressing,

"Gosh, do we have to do this six yard thing? It's a pain, really."

"I'm not so sure I like this look. It makes you look older"

That's an allusion to the cotton saris I love to wear to work and the fact that they take a while to tie because if they are cotton, they are starched and stiff. He is often still immersed in the newspaper as I ready to leave. When I'm all set to go, he will get up to check the car, the tires and my stuff. Even though the fellow who's cleaning the car would have seen it and said something if anything were the matter, that's not good enough for Diven who has to check for himself.

Then at the end of the work day, where intermittently I have got one or two calls from him

"What are you doing "?

"Working" standard reply and finally in the third or fourth call it will be

"When will you be home?"

"5ish"

"OK give me a call when you are nearly here and I'll put on the kettle"

That is so I can have my tea ready as soon as I get in.

And the evening would pass with us hardly seeing each others faces sometimes, both being involved in whatever we were doing but each knowing the other person was there, somewhere. I think that is the whole point, that the other person is there – somewhere.

We'd often argue over dinner, since something would invariably be wrong, the choice of food, the way it was cooked, the way it was served, the way the table was laid, something, anything.

Our day would end too in invariably the same fashion

"Diven, please put off the TV, I'm sleepy"

"In 10 minutes, I'm watching something important."

Something important meant Tennis, Cricket or the News. What is it with men? They love having the TV on even if they are dozing off in front of it and the remote in their hands. The minute you say

"Give me the remote"

The situation has turned into one with a potential for irritation, arguments and outright fights

So we too lived that way, nothing very different and nothing exciting.

So of course it follows that this is not my life. This is some kind of a weird farce I'm stuck in, a time warp, and it will suddenly, seamlessly and hopefully effortlessly, after all this lunacy and oddness, fall back into place, into normalcy.

Meanwhile the visits by the various well meaning and sympathetic persons are beginning to take their toll. There are so many people, relatives, some friends, even acquaintances, all of them coming to meet us, to commiserate in this time of grief. The faces and the names start to run into each other and their well meaning, oft-repeated platitudes begin to take on a drone like similarity. Its not that I don't appreciate their taking time off to come and console us, its just that they often do not really know what to say and I am closed in my mind to their words. My mind blurs the time of the day and I dread mealtimes, it is abhorrent to sit at the table on my own and face a meal with no Diven by my side and who ever else is there is a nuisance, an intrusion.

The nights are in some ways even worse. After these people have left, and the house is empty, when one could have some silence with one's thoughts, I have various relatives who have agendas all their own. There are some conversations, which will suddenly cease when I enter the room making it exceedingly evident that they in some manner concerned me. How do I put it across to them that it doesn't matter, they could have continued talking and I wouldn't have even known for I am never listening to them at all. They are concerned with so many things, the food, the cars, the running of the house, the future where as I am in a kind of zombie zone where none of this is registering and even if it is, it is surreal.

At present, keeping in mind that my loss is so recent, Aunt Leela is sleeping in my room. This is presumably meant to make me feel less alone and the fact that there is someone with me is supposed to help. To put it very simply, it doesn't. She is a well-meaning lady, somewhere in her late seventies and pleasant to a point. She worries about the fact that I am not eating much and considers food a remedy for most problems. She starts the day by planning breakfast, then goes on to plan lunch and then dinner and then the food for the next day. As can easily be understood, with all this preoccupation with edible objects she is a nice, healthy size. When she sleeps next to me on the big double bed she drops of to sleep within minutes of lying down and I lie there with my eyes wide open. Will it disturb her if I switch on the light and do some reading? Sleep doesn't seem to be coming my way easily and my mind is in a kind of overdrive and finally leaving her snoring in my bedroom I leave the room and sit in the silent corridor outside, near the verandah, hearing the wind in the trees and shedding tears in silence. Crying to myself, my misery silent and complete and total.

Why did this happen to me? There are so many people out there with the same disease that he had and some are 65 or seventy years old. They are doing ok and some aren't doing so ok but they are around.

So then, why my sweetie? Why him, he wasn't even old, he didn't even have any white hair in his head.

We were supposed to grow old together.

We were supposed to retire and then grow vegetables and watch the flowers bloom and live this nice, leisurely pace of life. I had always teased him that he would make a really handsome old man with his full head of hair turning salt and pepper and the ladies would still turn to look at him and he'd in turn reply that I would most probably be a ill tempered old lady. But God didn't even give him a chance to turn grey and took him away while he was still so young.

So now in my thoughts he will always be young. As I cry in the silence of the night I think how lucky he was and life was kind to him and how unfair to me. This may seem a foolish line of thought for someone who went so young but there is some truth to it. He was lucky for he always had me there, by his side, while I won't be so lucky. I will be alone. He died in my arms and if I could ever have asked him how he'd like to leave the world that would have been the way he would have liked to go.

There is some comfort in that. I dry my tears and go back to bed, listening to the sonorous sound of Aunt Leela's snoring and finally drop off into an uneasy slumber.

The first few days pass like this and slowly a kind of routine emerges since the world has other things to do. My world may have come to a grinding halt but the world around me hasn't. The sun still rises, the birds still sing in the trees; the day still goes on and ends in nightfall. Slowly, one by one, our guests and mourners go their own way and leave us to ourselves. So that leaves Aunt Leela, the servant and the maid and me. She busies herself in the running of the house and takes charge of everything in a manner which gives one the impression that I am a moron and incapable of performing even the most basic domestic tasks or in this case supervising them since there are servants to actually do them. She decides that the servant is cheeky, the maid is lazy and they are up to no good most of the time.

The issue here is, to my mind, that old ladies, who do not have much else to do with their time, make it their life's business to find faults with other peoples lives and doings. And this applies to everyone, the servants, the neighbors, and the younger generation today, the spouses of their various children and especially the relatives of their daughters in law or sons in law as the case may be. Of their own offspring there will be little mention since not much is wrong with them unless it is that the world had not done by them very fairly. That's bad luck you know or a lack of judgment on the part of the world at large. But us, as in daughter-in –law or kind of, that's oh well, well. There is no direct criticism, no cutting or nasty remarks for we are all too civilized for that but there is an undercurrent to many an innocent conversation.

As I start to return to the world of the living and begin to understand the magnitude of the tragedy, which has ripped my life apart, these things suddenly begin to impinge on my consciousness. All these days I had largely been unaware of these little poison barbs. As I review the situation around me certain facts begin to sink in. The servant is certainly not behaving very well mainly because he now sees that he has no authority figure to answer to, just a bunch of ladies. And the maid is having a field day with the household groceries with her light-fingered ways.

Human beings are selfish and self-centered creatures. In the midst of my sorrow and grief these things suddenly hold my attention and I am grateful for that. I need to get back to work and leave her to all this, give her free rein to do what she wants and not be there all the time to create this doubt as to who gives the orders in the house.

I am too tired to deal with all this as yet. Let her do it and we'll see later. Some mistakes are made I think, almost knowingly and at that point for me, this may have been one of them.

As I decide to go back to work my life takes on a distinct and at least somewhat familiar pattern. Take it one day at a time someone told me and believe me that is what keeps one sane. One day to decide about, what to wear, what to eat for breakfast, what to carry for lunch and what to then do for dinner. It's these little day-to-day things that work. My work is a different world. Its busy most of the time and even when it is not, it is businesslike and practical and the interactions with strangers who are completely indifferent to your personal life being too occupied with their own or their children's health issues. It will hopefully be a pleasant change from the all cosseting sympathy; the concerned looks and the careful watch which after a point starts to grate. I am not ungrateful, or at least I hope not and possibly that's a bit harsh but still true.

Standing in front on my wardrobe readying myself for resuming work I feel tired and drained and unwilling to face the world. But it has to be done and so I follow my routine of putting out my clothes before I go in for my bath. I look at my pretty saris, hanging in a line, all ironed and ready to wear and the blouses and underskirts arranged neatly in the drawers it suddenly seems like an immense effort to dress up. I pull out a pair of formal trousers and a plain full-sleeved cotton shirt. My days of six yards of fabric seem to have run into jeopardy. Wearing a sari will never be the same again.

Work is a relief. The comfortable routine of the patients, their parents, the juniors, the teaching sessions, the classes and clinics seem like a lifeline of familiarity in a now seemingly different and sometimes hostile world. Here, I don't feel so alone and so suddenly the odd person out. It has often been reiterated that work is the savior for grief and I totally ascribe to that philosophy. Work keeps you centered, gives a degree of normalcy, not to mention that it affords you an income and a degree of self esteem which in my case seems to all have taken a severe beating of late.

For suddenly my identity has changed. I was somebody's sweetheart and then his wife and then and always the most important person in his life. Now I'm not that any longer. So who am I? No other identity is ever that complete as that which encompasses you with your spouse. Whether people love each other or hate or are indifferent as is often the case with many marriages of late it still is your identity. You are so and so's wife or husband. Does this seem like a gross exaggeration or a woman's point of view and not applicable to the men or does it simply seems foolish. Quite apart from the fact that women may just emote more openly, I think men too feel a loss very keenly, a loss of identity as a couple.

You see, in society, you are a couple, the world functions in two's, in pairs. This is equally true and devastating for men too. I have known men who while going through a divorce have in addition to loneliness and social issues suddenly felt at a loss due to this. All your friends and social connections seem to be with people who are couples, its just a way of life over the years and the same people now though they try their best to call you over and make time for you and go that extra mile, its just not the same thing. It's a glaring deviation from norm, being on your own.

Work is good for me, time there passes and the day does not seem so long but the same cannot be said for the rest of my life. Life is shattered and the fragments impossible for me to put together into something viable. Home, that one word which holds a world of meaning, doesn't exist for me any longer. What is home? It's a place where there's someone waiting for you to get in. But I now have a house to go back to, four walls that seem to jump up and suffocate me. I often make detours, go to the marketplace, go over to friends and just make every effort to get in late.

I hate my house with so many people in it. It seems to have been taken over by aliens and I seem to have very little control over it and though earlier I had very little interest in the day to day running of it so long as it went on without hiccups now everything is an issue. I dimly get this feeling that I ought to make more of an effort to make my presence felt but the effort is quite beyond me.

It was nearly four weeks after his death that a small incident took on the proportions of a mountain in my already dazed mind.

A blazing hot day and humid with a hint of moisture in the air and I got home a bit earlier than I had been usually getting in. As I walk into the house through a front door which is open, something which should never happen in this city I can hear voices, laughter and animated conversation. Too tired to make the necessary social interactions I pause in the doorway and wonder where they are. The house isn't very big, it has only two bedrooms and these people are in my bedroom because it is the master bedroom and has a television and good air conditioner. Maybe this has been the norm for the past few days, I wouldn't know, but standing there all this is suddenly absolutely intolerable. I turn around and leave the house, driving off aimlessly.

"I need to take some control of my life", I think to myself as I drive out to one of the few green areas near the house. Without my even being aware of it my life seems to be run by some elders who take my quiescence with all this as a matter of course. And till now it hadn't really bothered me, or shall I say that I had been in a state of near blissful numbness to reality. Prior to all this there was only the two of us and whatever house help we had at a given time and though often quiet, the house had always held for me a sense of peace and relaxation. And now these relatives seem to have taken over and turned it into a kind of guesthouse in which I am a guest of sorts. I get out and go into the park like garden in the neighborhood and cry into my cupped hands.

That's all I seem to do whenever I am on my own. Shedding tears is supposed to make the heart lighter, why doesn't it work for me? I'm sick of my life, sick of this existence where everyday only seems to highlight my loss, my loneliness and my misery.

I don't want to do this anymore, don't want to try and be normal, and don't want to go on pretending that it's ok. It's not ok and as I sit there I realize that I don't think I want to live anymore. I've had enough and I can just end it all. I sit in this park, now oblivious to the heat and accepting my solution, my way out.

I am a doctor and so I can plan my end with some degree of knowledge and so I ponder over my options. Sleeping pills? Easy to do but not a very sure or foolproof method, could possibly be found a day later in coma or suchlike and be saved. That would be horribly embarrassing.

Ingestion of insecticide? Very effective, but so sickening, vomiting, maybe seizures, painful? Aware till how long? Propofol? That's how Michael Jackson had done it . . .that seems easy and painless. I am an expert at setting up I/V lines so that wouldn't be difficult only that it wouldn't maybe be possible to do on my hand and I'd have to do it on my foot. That's a bit messy but I could set up the whole thing very easily and that's it . . . who would find me? Do I want to do this now or later when all these people have left and I am on my own?

Somebody will find me, possibly the maid, I think to myself and then they'll inform my Dad . . . a dog barks in the distance and my thoughts come to a grinding standstill . . . . I come back to reality with a sudden and horrified understanding of what exactly is going through my mind. Its wrong, bad, positively evil to even allow such thoughts to enter your mind I tell myself and try and get a hold on myself.

I look around, it's hot, yes, but time will pass and the summer will be over, there will be cooler days and beautiful evenings and I am suddenly ashamed of myself. It's a sin to contemplate ending life, a crime, and a hateful lack of gratitude for the many things that I do have in my life and it is against Gods wishes. Though few us are overtly religious I think we all still believe in the presence of the almighty or in someone or some power bigger than merely human who seems to hold the world in place and at least guide it, if not actually run it.

I shake myself out of my morbid reverie and promise myself that never, ever am I going to allow my thoughts to meander down that particular path again. Life is precious. This something we say over and over again, part of the teaching of my profession and also to my mind an innate and indestructible belief. It's a gift, which we are given, to make the most of, and we owe it to ourselves and the people around us to do the best by it.

So what if it doesn't always seem to do the best by us?

God has his ways and we have to accept them. In this frame of mind and now determined in a still somewhat shaky manner I head home with the firm decision that I am going to try and take control of my life and start by sorting out my problems one by one and not focus on the negatives but the positive things in my life. I do not at present have any monetary problems, I have a job and work which I love and which in addition to the financed does afford me some respect in society, I have some very good friends and I have my family. All in all I have a great deal to be thankful for.

On this note I decide to head to Kiya's, rather than going home, for a cup of tea, and maybe a cigarette, should she permit it.

We all have friends and acquaintances but some of us are blessed to have friends who we can be sure will always be there by our side no matter what. My friends and especially one of them is in my thoughts as I drive home. Kiya and I, we grew up in this small town where there wasn't a great deal to entertain young people and that wasn't the age of the mobile phones and the Internet. Next door neighbors a going to the same school and later the same college for a short while we are friends with a long history. We studied in the same school, exchanged book and comics as teenagers, learned about boys, life and marriage together. I doubt if I could even recall all that we have shared over the years with accuracy, we've been a part of each others lives for what seems like forever and if anyone ever gave me a bit of information regarding her which I was unaware of I'd know it to be a lie. We have no secrets from each other for there is a degree of trust and caring that negates there being any reason to keep things to oneself. We have the ease of a friendship that can come only with long years of knowing, caring, nurturing and accepting, crying on each others shoulders in bad times and laughing together in the good ones. We are not judgmental of each other but that is not to say that we do not criticize each other, in fact I'd say that she is sometimes my fussiest critic. That may be with regards to what I wear and how I look and down to the way I conduct my life and myself.

"Heavens, why do you get your hair cut so short? You look like a plucked chicken. Its too harsh, too unfeminine"

"I like is short, its convenient" that's me, defensive, justifying my look.

Or it can be

"For Gods sake go and get yourself waxed. You seem to have hair everywhere except on your head" This is another one on my hair and then there are sundry ones like

"Oh, please where did you get that particular outfit? Give it away, to your maid, I'm sure she will love it."

"Who got that sari for you? I'm sure you didn't buy it yourself, your taste really cant be that bad" for a sari she is absolutely sure I did buy myself.

"That bag is horrendous. We really must get you a new one"

Kiya is a good dresser, her taste impeccable whether it be clothes or jewelry or the way her house is done.

And on the other hand me, I'm not fussed so long as I am neat and clean and my clothes are like decent and appropriate to the occasion. Loving a bit of bling on occasion and getting an earful from my best friend used to be a part of life.

For all that we are friends we are as different as chalk from cheese. Kiya is fair, a trifle plump and very pretty and I was always somewhat an ugly duckling, tall and thin and dark. Kiya was married early and had her kids even before I completed my childhood dream of becoming a doctor. As a matter of fact, over the years we may have had times when we lived life with completely different priorities and responsibilities but our relationship has to my mind been steady and rock solid. Many a day now when my mind balks at the thought of going home to a house without Diven I go over to her house and just while away time before heading home. It helps, I talk and she listens or she criticizes and I pretend to listen and that how it has often been. The familiarity of our conversations has a comforting feeling and to my mind at least there is something is life, a relationship, which simply cannot change, come what may. I know she is always there for me, to listen when I talk, to give advise which often goes unheeded and to understand a great deal of what is not said and need not be put into words.

As I now sit in her home using her as a sounding board and try to sort out my thoughts, I wonder about God too. I had for years been going to the temple every Thursday morning and offering prayers or just sitting there and listening to the hymns being sung by devotees. Had always believed that it left me with a sense of peace and with a feeling of goodwill towards humanity and made me a better person. But ever since this I haven't gone. I don't believe in God any longer. If there were a God why would he do things like this? Why would he be so unfair? I stop my thoughts right there and make up my mind that I am going to fight this depression which seems to be getting its grip on me, this slow slide into despondency and lethargy which has crept up on me.

I finish my tea and cookies and head home.

Over the next few days I make a conscious effort to look at life in a more positive way. I aim to dress better and look nicer which at this point is rather difficult since I have lost some weight and being fairly slim to begin with my look is somewhat gaunt. And I have decided that when I wake in the morning I will tell myself that

"Today is going to be a good day"

"I will not be negative"

"I will think about how much he cared for me and loved me and the good times we had together"

This works, you know. If you start the day with a conviction that it will be good and that you will make a conscious effort to see the best in things, things do look better.

Like a self-fulfilling prophecy of the human mind. If I were to say

"I'm doomed"

It's likely I would be.

And as to the things I have yet to set right in life, those I will take on, one by one.

In our country everything has associated with it a whole set if rituals which are 'important' and 'must be done'. Be it a birth or a wedding, a new house or a new job there are many rules to follow. I think the weddings are the worst but deaths are not so far behind and if this statement may seem like a macabre attempt at humor that's inadvertent. You have ceremonies on the fourth or the thirteenth day and something else on the fortieth day. These are all meant to provide for peace of the departed soul and let them leave their earthly ties. It is believed in Hinduism that the soul hovers close to its loved one or to its earthly and materialistic ties for about 40 days and then departs to the other world. In unnatural deaths the soul may not be able to find peace and continue on its journey but may stay near its loved ones and not be at rest.

I really wouldn't know how all this works and unto this point in life had never paid any attention to it. When my mother died a few years ago we went through all the right things at the right times as a matter of course and didn't agonize over the finer details. Now it seems every little thing has a huge and significant meaning and must be done right. Probably these came to be so that for a few weeks people would be kept busy preparing for some religious ceremony or the other and the immediate period of grief would be dulled.

But grief doesn't follow a pattern of reducing with time or fading in a systematic manner. Days can pass in which one is composed and them some very trivial day to day occurrence can take you right back to the bottom of that pit, back to the moment it happened and break you all over again.

Crying to sleep or crying as I try to fall off to sleep seems to have become a way of life with me. Sleep is often elusive and I think with envy of all the people who fall off to sleep immediately as they lie down. I used to be like that, lie down and within fifteen minutes I'd doze off.

Now I toss and turn, and worry and cry often late into the night, my heart as bleak as my life, a bottomless pit, dark and joyless.

In The Silence

"It is strange how silence roars in my ears,
Where I used to yearn for it, it now deafens me"

Time has this undeniable and inexorable way of passing on. It stops for no one and writes change that for many of us can be difficult or unacceptable. Acceptance of fate or whatever we call as 'kismet' in our country is something I have come to discern as a great answer to many unfortunate occurrences. We are programmed in India to accept the worse as 'something that had to happen', 'that was written by a power that is divine' and that it was 'destiny'. Possibly it makes dealing with calamity and grief easier; there may be some comfort in accepting that it wasn't in human hands to change it. But living with it is another thing altogether.

Two months have gone by since life dealt me a blow enough to shatter my existence into miniscule shards of pain and I still struggle every single day to put it together to make some kind of sense, wondering if it will ever be possible for me to really live again, possible to smile, possible to be happy or if not that at least content. Things have changed and even as I make decisions about day-to-day trivialities I seem to try forever to decide whether I am doing it right. Decision-making is not my forte in life; I am not good at it. Very much an 'if and but' personality, sometimes to the point of dithering on very trivial issues, unable to make up my mind or o put my foot down and often taking a 'wishy washy' stance, that's me.

Take the matter of the manservant, as an example. Very early after being on my own I was aware that keeping him was not a good idea because, for one we did not have enough work to keep him busy and hence out of trouble, and also because the absence of a man in the house led to his becoming sometimes insolent and often rude. I didn't really face this very much but Aunt Leela did, and any sign of suspected insubordination led to her raising her voice and attempting to shout him down into subservience. It didn't really work and probably made him behave even more badly and led to his vanishing for hours on end for some errand which could be done in much less time and making her wait for her meals.

Her obsession with food was something he played on, turning unavailable at mealtimes, serving up yesterdays leftovers, leaving the dishes in the sink for hours and so on and so forth. A head on confrontation was inevitable and I could see it coming and had I been a more decisive and in control person I could simply have sent him on his way. But I watched it play on to its inevitable end as one day he got into a fight with someone in the colony and a neighbor came to the house to complain about his behavior, giving Aunt Leela a godsent opportunity to list his endless misdemeanors and raise a complete shindig with the onlookers having a field day. She pushed him out of the house, shouting all the while and collecting all the people she could and finally after a great deal of unpleasantness on both sides his account was settled and he went his way.

Ditto the maid, she apparently made off with thousands of rupees, which were there in the house. That I was unaware of any such amount of money lying in the house would have made no difference, and my defending her would have been futile had I even attempted to do so. That lady, the maid, no matter how sinister and dishonest she was made out to be, had been the one who had spent many hours caring for my husband during his illness and for that alone I would have let her go without unpleasantness. But no, there was a great deal of mudslinging about

"These people making off with money at the slightest opportunity" and

"God knows what all else she must have picked up over the months" and

"How would you know? You are never here".

That is obviously meant to put me in my place. At the end of all this, tired of our making a spectacle of ourselves as a regular feature it seemed, I took her aside, gave her some extra money and told her to leave.

So now we have a new lady house help who is a stranger to me. That is something that has always struck me as being amazing the ease with which you can get various kinds of house help. Of course their caliber is quite often distinctly suspect, but they are available, cooks, someone to wash clothes, someone to swab the floors and do the cleaning, or someone to just do it all.

Since it was easier left to Aunt Leela to sort out I did just that. She was convinced that we would be better off with someone older, middle aged to be precise rather than the younger ones we had just got rid of. Her logic was something like

"She is likely to be more reliable"

"Pray, why so?"

I feel inclined to ask but refrain from doing so

"And less likely to be flighty" she goes on

I give in as I always do, what's the point in arguing anyway?. So we get this lady to work in the house. Her name is Geeta and she is around fifty-five or so, quiet and unassuming on the face of it and for some reason she gets on my nerves. She is sloppy and untidy and the kitchen suffers the worst of it and I am, for my part, convinced that she is definitely likely to stay for I can't imagine anyone trying to tempt her away. Lets see how it goes I think and put it on a slow burner as I have more pressing concerns.

Other more important issues to take care of, I think to myself as I leave our maid to her activities in the kitchen with some trepidation. Aunt Leela has been giving me not so subtle hints

"I've been away too long, need to think about going back home" and again

"I think you'll be ok on your own now"

"You really don't need my any longer"

Contrary to what it may seem, these are not indicators of any desire on her part to go back to her home. No, they are actually a way of of asking me to contradict her claims. What is expected of me in reply is something to the tune of

"No, please don't go, I need you here, I can't manage on my own"

And in a way it's true for she has been a savior for me in this time of need. I would have been lost without her and now I wonder what to say. I am unsure how I will manage without her for I have never lived on my own. Strange to reach the age of 48 years without having ever lived alone, never lived in a hostel, never done anything totally solo so to say. I studied from home and then got married. Just as simple as that and that must is the story of millions of women in India. May be a record of sorts in this day and age but now what?. My mind blanks out a bit, oh, isn't that something I seem to do an awful lot these days, go blank? The thought of coming back to an empty house gives me the jitters. So I will what? Lock up the house when I go to work. Well, obviously. And then when will the maid come to do the cleaning and the rest of the housework? In the morning before I leave, but that time I am getting ready for work and I cant supervise her, or in the evening when I am not even sure what time I will be getting in.

My routine is likely to go haywire all over again and the other cause for concern, she doesn't seem very trustworthy and everything is lying without lock and key. I will have to keep track of the maid, the chauffeur, the cooking, the food, the clothes, the garbage, everything.

Many confusing thoughts spin around my head and dance into chaos. I wasn't sure initially whether I'd like having her living with me but all the same Aunt Leela has kept me sane the past few weeks. If nothing else her presence ensures the house is not a silent mausoleum I return to at the end of the day and also she presently ensures so many things, some order, some routine, someone to talk to, the meals cooked, the house cleaned and the house help supervised.

And her near constant obsession with certain things, food for one and the various ailments she imagines she suffers from, provides for a source of some amusement and often irritation in my life.

On a busy Monday I get a call from home, the maid mutters down the line

"Memsahib is not feeling well. She has been taken ill"

My heart sinks, imagining her falling and having a heart attack. In view of my recent association with hospitals my nerves don't handle anyone being unwell very calmly.

"Oh God how bad is she? She hasn't even been able to come to the phone"

I ask the maid even as my palms sweat with fright.

"No, no she is not that bad. Her tummy is bad and she is in the toilet. She just wants you to get some medicine and come home early"

I am not amused. My nerves settle and I heave a sigh of relief.

This was just one of them, her varied ailments, I mean. She had issues with her back which she had sprained at some point in time, which could mean anything from five to thirty years and it still played up off and on. And the chest pain which is the master of all complaints at giving people a hard time at any given time, too often serious to be underplayed. When will people realize that aging is a natural process and the doctors don't have the answers to everything least of all to the various joint aches and backaches of old women?

It's tiring to sort out some real or imagined illness all the time. In addition to this she feels let down because I don't see the need to consult the neurologist, the orthopedician, the cardiologist or the physician at every little twinge she feels. I begin to realize too that she is, at the end of the day, an old lady and in doing what she is for me, she is putting herself out a great deal. It isn't easy for her to cope either and now, maybe she needs to go back to her own life.

I accept the inevitable and decide that all things said and done, what with our differences and various other ups and downs, the bottom line is that though it does help me, her being here, the time has now come for her to leave.

As I dither in my usual indecisive fashion, unable to formulate an appropriate reply to her on the face of it 'not meant to be taken seriously statements', which are closer to the truth than is comfortable, fate again takes a turn at playing with our lives. The next day Aunt Leela gets a phone call from her home. Her husband is not keeping too well and she is needed there quite urgently. She will have to leave.

Possibly at the time of her departure she had a better idea than I did what I would be looking at. Before she leaves she tells me in detail about various little things in my own house, where the crockery and cutlery should be, what should be locked up, how the gas is to be ordered, the phone number of the person to contact in case the inverter plays up and many such nuggets of information.

I try and absorb all this and am surprised to hear
"And 'Uttran' comes on at 9.30 pm on Colors"
Uttran?? What is that?
Then I realize that she is talking about the soap she watches with religious regularity and by virtue of the fact that I am often sitting with her late evening, she thinks I am following it too. I hadn't even realized the name of the serial and far from following it I am invariably lost in my own thoughts and oblivious to these highly made up and complicated TV characters in our now numerous shows. So far removed from reality they sometimes seem like someone's misguided fantasies. Anyway, I think, nodding at every instruction, it is good of her.

Suddenly
"Don't sit around in the house all the time. Go out and do something interesting"
"Meet up with people some more"
"Keep track of the maid. She is light fingered"
"Don't keep money in the house. It attracts trouble"

Touched and somewhat remorseful that I am looking forward to her departure, I go see her off at the airport, as I know she does have a tough time walking a lot and this is going to be a tiring day for her. As I hug her and wish her goodbye she has tears in her eyes and "Bless you" and she is walking down the long stretch to the airport departure lounge. Goodbye Aunt Leela.

After she has left it takes me a day or two to just settle in again. I am a stranger in my own home. Locking the house to leave for work in initially daunting. Have I left the iron on? What about the air conditioner? There was no electricity when I left the house and there will be fire and. . . . it goes on and on in my head. Creating problems where none exist and then mulling over them. It's all in the mind sometime.

Coming back to an empty house is the toughest thing to do.

When I drive back home at end of the day I am reluctant to get there. Reluctant to walk in to a quiet empty house, reluctant to sit alone in the long evenings and to eat alone. The silent rooms seem to mock me with their tidiness, everything in place and neat and clean. No mess in the bathroom, no towels lying around, no ashtray overflowing with butts, no smell of 'agarbatti' in the air, no one to put on the kettle for my tea and no one waiting for me to get home. The maid gets in soon after me so I don't have long to brood at this time but I don't like her and that too is a thorn in my side. She does whatever she has to do, the cooking, gives me my dinner, cleans up and leaves. She will come again in the morning for the rest of the chores. After she has gone, I lock up and check all the doors and windows and face the endless night.

After darkness sets in, the days work done, is when reality starts to sink in. I wander through the house picturing it in my minds eye with him in it, Diven watching TV, smoking in the verandah, bent over the crossword puzzles he so loved to solve, dozing in front of the television with the remote in his hand and sleeping. These images haunt me and I turn to his wardrobe and run my hands over his clothes, his things, as they were when he last left them. Nothing changed, nothing handled by anyone, his scent lingers here, a mixture of cologne and soap and a smell, which is essentially his. Standing there in the semidarkness I feel angry, hurt, confused, lost. Feel like screaming my rage at the world and at him.

Where are you? I ask him.

"You have to be close by somewhere, near me, you can't be gone forever".

Some words seem so harsh now, forever is one of them and another one is never, I'll never see him again. Never? How am I going to live with that? Somehow it has to be done.

It's not as though I don't have support or friends. I have Kiya and I have my father, two people who are concerned and constantly trying to keep up my spirit. I have other friends too and they too rally around me but Kiya calls regularly and Dad, he does so much that I worry about his health. He is not young and often now to me appears frail. He meets me for lunch every week or 10 days coming halfway to town while I go halfway. He calls, he attempts to cheer me up and make me more outgoing and I

"What are you doing?" Dad asks me on one evening as I sit in the house, all alone

"Nothing"

"You have that plaza close to your house, Get up, go there and I'll call you in half an hour. Don't sit around aimlessly"

The plaza is a small gallery of shops close to where I stay. Hardly any thing there but still there are people and an eatery or two.

"I want him back Dad, I can't go on like this"

"He's gone 'beta', to a place from where you can't return"

In tears, I still made the effort to go to the plaza and while away some time.

Some incidents will stay in our minds indelibly marked, forever etched in memory. One such turning point is my life was strange and undeniable and I'm still not sure of its credibility. In the past few weeks I had received several books with the theme being related to miracles, seeing God and witnessing or communicating with the other world. I had 'Gods miracles' and 'On the other side' and 'Where do our loved ones go after they die' and though I hadn't fully read any of them, I had leafed through them and they played on my mind.

Most of these books, for they are meant to console, focus on some kind of communication with people whom we have lost and I don't know still whether I really would believe in this without reservation. The human mind is strange and I think capable of deceiving its own waking self in a kind of self- preservation is what I would find more plausible. We are capable of fooling ourselves into believing in miracles and god men and many things, which in the present frame of mind I was too.

Finding myself often unable to sleep till very late in the night and being groggy and tired in the day seemed to have become a day-to-day event. In addition I now found myself troubled by migraines, a malady to which I have been predisposed for years. The headaches suddenly surfaced and I found myself often lying in the center of my big double bed in the middle of the night, holding my head in pain with my eyes squinted against the light if it was on or with one of those eye patches that the airlines give at night to cover them. Applying balm till my skin burned, taking pain medicines and some antacids I tired myself to sleep on many nights.

On one such occasion I decided that I would take a sedative and sleep as I knew the pain only truly settles after a good nights sleep. Contrary to popular belief being a doctor does not mean one is fond of self-medicating though I dare say there are plenty of those too. Looking at the medicines, sedatives basically, and choosing one I decided to take a half tablet being paranoid about sleeping too long or being hungover the next day. I think half the reason sleeping pills work is that once you have swallowed one, you are so convinced that you will sleep, that you do.

And so did I. I shut off the lights and dozed off. And then. . . . . .

A state of half awareness, a feeling of not being alone in the room, of there being someone there with me. Not quite awake and not asleep either I opened my eyes in the darkened room and saw quite clearly the burning cigarette but a few feet away. In my hazy half awake state I think to myself

"Why is he smoking in the dark" and I uttered his name *"Diven"*

It was like a split second, drawn out in time, for in the same instant reality hits like a hammer. And the time it takes me to come to sitting up in bed, the moment is gone. The light of the cigarette, that feeling of a presence. It's vanished. There is nobody there.

What happened? Did I imagine the whole thing? Am I going crazy? Hallucinating?

Did I imagine it? The feeling was so strong that the mood stayed, lingered on in my mind. I went off to sleep with a feeling of comfort, which stayed with me over the day. I felt he was close to me, somewhere near me and that he'd take care of me or at least see that I didn't come to serious harm. To try and explain this to anyone wasn't really possible so I didn't even really try. I'm rational enough to understand that I could have imagined it all under the effect of the sedative medication, but the feeling was so strong that I am not willing to accept that explanation and I do not have a better one so I will leave it at that. Often I have been able to smell incense as though someone has lit it in the house or hear the distinctive click of a lighter in the silence of the nights when I am alone but now I just accept it and do not question it. We do rationalize every event but some things can be left to the heart to understand and not to the mind to analyze.

I was told at one religious ceremony that the spirit of the departed persons lingers for at least 40days and so I am willing now to cling to that belief that he is still somewhere near me and can guide my actions. This total lack of ability to take the onus of my own decisions is still worrying but now I talk to him and let him decide. At the end of the day I took to conducting conversations with him and then deciding what to do. It helps just to think that someone is listening.

The first issue I needed to deal with was the maid or house help whatever word is acceptable. I did not like her but till now

I had made no effort to replace her. I wonder how I should deal with her and how I should go about getting rid of her. She is tardy, unreliable and actually quite cunning I realize with a new insight into the situation. I leave the house for work in the morning and am not back till late evening and she realizes that I am in fact quite dependent on her for most of the practical issues like food being cooked, the house being cleaned, the clothes being washed and whatever else may be needed. Her method of dealing with this new aspect now that Aunt Leela is not there to ask for a raise

"I do everything and money doesn't buy much any longer. For Rs. 100 you can get nothing. The onions, the tomatoes see how expensive everything is"

From inside my head I can see myself give in to this demand today and then every time it is made. I think to myself that I can manage; yes I can manage and deliver the ultimatum

"No, I cannot raise your salary. You may leave if it does not suit you"

She has been pushed into a corner now. She backs off

"No, no, I can not leave you like this, all on your own. I will manage somehow . . . maybe next month we can see what is to be done"

But I have now found some courage so I tell her to leave. She leaves in a huff, muttering to herself and I am convinced that I will be blacklisted in the list of the 'would be helps'. Sometimes nowadays I surprise myself by being an aggressor where my temperament is largely amicable. I am pleased with myself but now I have the additional headache of the housework too. I think it does me some good though; leaves me tired, physically exhausted and falling off to sleep. Since the night I saw that burning light in my bedroom I have slept better, more at peace with myself, whatever the logic maybe.

Preparing meals can be a pleasure, an art of creation, done with élan and flair or it can be a mechanical chore done with the intent of getting it over and done with. Domesticity was never my strong point and depending on my own resourcefulness and cooking skills starts to have a depressing effect. There is silence all the time and in all these days since Aunt Leela left the television in the living room had not been switched on. I have no desire to watch the news with its endless controversies of violence, politics or even sports. Somehow nothing seems to hold my interest and I seem to be sinking into this abyss of indifference to life. I do recognize this and make a concentrated effort to hold on but the silent evenings and the dark nights tell on me. Looking in the mirror in the mornings I see a stranger everyday, an unsmiling countenance, thin nearly gaunt face and the greying hair. Grey hair has suddenly appeared in streaks in my dark hair. They don't really bother me and in fact I feel they add a touch of maturity and in any case I feel old, really old and drained.

The night is always the darkest before dawn, or so they say, and I touched those darkest moments now. At this point on my own I began to realize that negativity could truly corrode the soul. Every belief, every conviction shakes and life is insecure, confidence ebbs and the spirit is weak and sad. Taking it one day at time I live my life in a slow caricature of living, going to work, coming back home, completing the necessary activities and sleeping only to go to work again the next day. Socializing is beyond me and I haven't even seen Kiya in weeks.

But there is a dawn and if we just hold on long enough it will come to us. I decide that bringing is someone to do some of the housework may be a first step in helping myself. And so I start the process of taking some control of my life. Here, in our colony, and I presume elsewhere too, it is not difficult to get part time help though what you get is a kind of blind date, never know how it will turn out. I tell the security guard that I am looking for a new maid and he should be on the lookout for me. This is one way of doing it and the other way is to tell one of the other maids in the colony that you need one. There seems to be a quick network of communication in this lot of people, a working advertisement service. My neighbors, an elderly couple who are living on their own, seem to have a good maid. She is hard working from what I can make out and cheerful too, often chirping a greeting to me as I open the door in the early morning to pick up the newspaper. They, Mr. and Mrs. Khanna, are nice too, offering to send her over to make 'chappatis' for me should I so wish. I realize that I hardly know them having maybe visited them once when we moved in here.

Yet another of my lacunae, I hardly know the neighbors and my knowledge of them was in any case second hand coming as it did from my husband. He had more time on his hands and a great deal more curiosity too. 'Nosy' I used to say as he seemed to know the oddest secrets about people, who got along and who didn't,

"Mr. Mehra has a girlfriend" and

"Mr. Kapoor goes behind the general store to smoke" and

"I think he is gay" for some other poor soul.

A fleeting smile touches my lips as I recall some of the nasty ones about the Khannas

"Those two, the Khanna's, they are really miserly. I tell you she counts the 'chappatis' they give to that girl who is working for them. And they never pay her on time"

"The electrician was complaining that Mr. Khanna made him wait two weeks before he paid him"

"They are both retired people, what do they need so much money for?"

The last with reference to the fact that they regularly hold some kind of tuitions for school going children in the neighborhood, in their house, and make some money. I smile as I think of all this, suddenly amused recalling the acerbic remarks.

I decline their offer of the maid's services but request them to help me find one. They are very forthcoming and I end up having a cup of tea at their house. They are reassuring and say I will find someone soon.

After a day or two the security guard for the colony says there are one or two ladies who are willing to do the work, and when would you like to see them.

"On Sunday morning", I reply, dreading having to deal with two or more ladies and trying to work out their worth to me and haggling over the final payment. I could gladly and easily pay the going rate or more, but one this issue one thing stands clear. If I do not attempt to bargain for a lower price, if I don't make any attempt to push my advantage and establish my superiority in a way, then I am likely to be not granted much respect in the eyes of these workers and as such I could expect trouble. So I kind of steel myself for this one.

She is a pleasant surprise. Only one lady shows up on the given Sunday morning and she is, from the look of her, either Nepalese or what we call as 'pahari', belonging to the mountains. She turns out to be from Nepalese stock though she has never been to Nepal. Seemingly soft spoken, she is young and pretty which appeals, and she claims that she is a good cook. I have already decided that I like the look of her as I question her

"What is your name?"

"Sangeeta" she replies with a smile.

Though I was to later discover that this was not her given name which was a more complicated 'Surajkala', a much older and more traditional name, and she had chosen to give me this name for she felt it was nicer, her habit of smiling at every query was pleasing and I didn't do much by way of checking her credentials which is actually often a mistake. Repeatedly we hear about people being robbed or even murdered and still we don't learn.

So Sangeeta started to come for work. She is still with me, 3 years later, and I have had no reason to regret employing her. She comes in the morning and does sundry jobs and serves breakfast and prepares lunch for me to carry should I want any and then she leaves. I go off to work and after I am back she comes over in the evening around 6.30 pm for the evening stint. She effectively does all the housework, she cooks, and she does the clothes. Initially I did keep a close eye on her but over time my faith in her capabilities has grown and now she is very much a part of my household.

And yes, in accordance with her claims, she is a very good cook. She enjoys cooking and is willing to try new and exotic recipes and is fond of nonvegetarian cooking. As we kind of settle in to each other, I find her a talkative and intelligent person. Though she claims to have studied upto 8th grade, she cannot write a single line and her reading skills are very basic. She can however keep track of kitchen accounts with surprising accuracy and remembers every little detail. Another example of wasted potential in our country for girls of a certain social class are rarely educated at all and married off rather young. She is in her early thirties and has a sixteen-year-old daughter and a son a year younger. She resides nearby and is quite happy leaving a little on the later side as she says it is very close by.

Most maids coming to the larger apartments and residential colonies will leave by around 7 to get back to nearby villages or slums in which they live. Here in India, you can find a slum right next to the luxury apartments in residential areas, the same way as you can see a Mercedes and a Bullock cart at a village crossing. So she is around till 9 or so and definitely takes the edge of the long evenings.

And she talks. She is a chatterbox and loves to gossip.

"Did you know that the lady in the apartment across the road is having an affair with her brother in law?

Her husband discovered them and he beat him up, the other man. Me, I think he should have beaten her up"

In addition to being up to date in her gossip, Sangeeta also has firm and clear opinions about most anything. Her nonstop chatter punctuates the background as she cooks and cleans and goes about the house. Can't say I have much interest in the affairs of the ladies in the colony but I listen and even add my two bits sometimes to keep her going. She has a pleasant singsong intonation and intermittently uses English words too.

"Very expensive", this is for her kid's school uniform, which you have to buy from the school itself and "Understand?" to me when I am not paying attention and she makes a joke with innuendo.

"I do" I nod to her as I finally start to relax in my house, my evenings now easier to spend and the food tasting better and things starting to fall in place. She plays on my emotions all the time, sometimes deliberately and often without intent.

Picking up a framed picture of my husband and me taken a few years ago and with both of us smiling happily she comments

"You both look very happy. Sahib was very handsome and so fair. Life is very sad"

Yes I can understand she plays on my emotions, but it hardly matters. A lot of her song and dance is just prelude to her asking

"May I have an advance on my salary" which will be a demand for just a sum of Rs. 500 or a thousand, which she will repay, later but still I like to hear her little stories and enjoy her obvious attempts at flattering me.

She is also very good at the practical things, which can lead to hiccups in day-to-day functioning. She is well acquainted with electricians, plumbers, and the television mechanics and even with people who can do basic work on cars and all kind of sundry odd jobs.

Our routine suits me and my life begins to settle to some extent. I have no social life to speak of at this point, not because I'm not invited anywhere its just that I am not ready to fact the world, the social world, as yet. Work doesn't count, it is there but it doesn't really intrude in my self. Hence life becomes a bit of a limbo, a kind of a cocoon in which I am going from day to day my life colorless, meaningless and often excruciatingly lonely.

I look into the mirror and don't really know whom I see there. I have become a stranger to myself, my face looks thin, my hair is longer now and the grey is evident and I look as old as I am. I need to do something about this I think to myself and am unable to take that first step to salvage my existence and so life drags on in monotony. Lethargy drags at my feet and dulls my brain.

I do so need to pull myself up by the bootstraps, but how?

The Exercise 'Mantra'

"Exercise is good not just for the body,
But also for the heart and the soul"

Winter in Delhi, does not come in with a bang. It creeps in insidiously, the blazing blistering sun giving way to a more mellow and pleasant warmth, the days getting shorter, the nights lengthening. Unlike the mountain regions there is no real fall, we just go from summer to winter. And winter in Delhi is a pleasure, outdoors activities abound, get togethers are planned, the festive season sets in and the mood is merry.

I watch, an outsider it seems, to the social activity around me.

Birthdays hurt and the anniversary is just another day. Friends and family are kind and I get so many calls on his birthday with everyone understanding that it will be a tough day. Memories come in a rush, the birthdays over the years, some good, and some silly. Giving gifts over the years and some nearly forgotten memories. Thinking of some silly ones I shed tears even though I smile at my thoughts. On every birthday of his I recall asking what he'd like to have, for he was a really fussy person sometimes and something bought of my own choice was likely to not be met with great pleasure. I am easier to please, flowers and chocolates would do or even a single red rose. Among the birthday gifts I got for him over the years two in the recent years particularly come to my mind as I sit and brood. Just prior to one birthday I was travelling abroad and so I asked if I could get him something, which is not easily available in India. Prompt reply

"I would like a Cigar – Cutter"

Clueless I ask, "What on earth is that? I mean it sounds like something to cut a cigar with but what exactly does it do that's so special?"

So I got an explanation in much detail regarding the civilized way of smoking a cigar. I hadn't ever seen him smoke a cigar. So I have to get this thing and cigars too, is that it?

"No, no, you just get the cutter"

So on the last leg of my journey, which was in France I start looking for a cigar cutter. In France they have these shops called 'Tobacconists' or 'Le Tabac' which sell all kinds of tobacco products and in one of these I go about hunting for this odd gift. No luck, a lot of fancy lighters, all kinds of pipes and tobaccos with flavors and aromas and cigarette cases and all the paraphernalia a smoker could want. In my opinion the last kind of gift I should buy should be something associated with smoking since I have been very insistent that he stop doing it, but that argument didn't hold any weight with him. Looking at all the beautiful objects in this place I decide to buy a momento lighter just in case I am unable to get the cigar cutter, as it doesn't appear to be an easy thing to find.

Finally on a stopover at Schiphol, the airport at Amsterdam, where I see a cigar shop I try again. Language is an obstacle as they speak no English but finally after pointing at the cigars and miming a chopping action I am shown the cutters. Funny looking thing it has two rings, places to put your thumb and index finger, and a central bigger zone where the end of the cigar is held to 'cut' it. Looks like a kind of tiny instrument of torture, and really not an attractive object. Seeing the price I am tempted to stand by my initial stance that I was not able to get it. But then, as usual, pleasing him is a priority, and it is a birthday gift, so I buy it. Well that was one.

And another one, this one also peculiar. When I asked him

"What would you like for your birthday this year?"

I am happily informed.

"I know what I want, but its expensive. I doubt if we can afford it"

"Doesn't matter, tell me and tell me the approximate cost too, then we'll see"

It always did amaze me the way Diven would have this fixation with certain objects, obsessing over them to a point where it seemed that they gave him so much pleasure that it would please me to be able to gift them to him.

"A Big Bertha"

Sounds like the name of a cow to me, so I just keep quiet knowing that I will put my foot in my mouth if ask. And he waits for me to ask so he can make fun of my ignorance.

"Yes, ok" I reply after a while when no further explanation seems forthcoming.

"It's a driver, you know"

"Oh boy, curiouser and curiouser" as they said in Alice in Wonderland I think as I absorb this comment, totally at sea when suddenly the light dawns. Obviously wood, iron, steel, titanium, yet another fixation. Golf and its add ons be it balls, tees, caps, gloves, shoes are in plenty in our house.

All these things, the Big Bertha, the cigar cutter, the fancy Zippos are here, right beside me, I think to myself and the person who loved this junk so much, he is gone. And I decide, sitting there and in that moment, that though tears are never far from the surface on these once special days for me I am not going to be sad and I am not going to cry. I have a different line of thought today and am focused on how he would want me to be. Certainly not drab and dreary and moaning all the time.

"Smile baby, the world looks better that way. And anyway you have a million dollar smile"

I can almost hear him as he says that, which would happen every time I was in the doldrums about something, which wasn't very rare.

I am not going to cry. He wouldn't have wanted that.

I can still get a cake of some sort, if I want to, I think. I need not say anything to anyone about it but I want to remember him on his birthday with good memories, not tears.

I don't want to have anyone over either for they may find all this peculiar and start to wonder if I am losing my marbles. I go to the supermarket and get a small chocolate cake from the bakery and then decide to give it to Sangeeta for her kids after taking a piece for myself. I do not tell her any special significance and she is always happy to have something nice to give to her kids.

The festive season in India is long and protracted, and fascinating. We love elaborate gestures, extravagant gifts and huge big dos. Dussehra and Diwali are the two big festivals in India coming within three weeks of each other. If one were to look for a festival similar to Christmas in India, Diwali would be it. Though it has religious connotations it is largely a time of merry making, giving gifts, throwing parties and having a good time all in all. For ten days before the actual day of Diwali the spirit of the city will be gay, there is shopping and all the market places are jam packed with people buying gifts and clothes for the family and friends. Over the years it is also a very commercial and business oriented enterprise with this very justified opportunity to send incentives to work associates. Partying late into the night is the norm and another favorite aspect of this season is the organization of card playing sessions. All variety of people will play cards; card games will range from mere social ones with family gatherings to big time serious games with mind-boggling stakes. Cards are always played before the Diwali day and never on the holiday itself. The day of the festival is marked with the worship of the Goddess Lakshmi and lighting the house with lamps, the 'diyas' or 'deepaks' from which the festival gets its formal name 'Deepawali' or the 'Festival of lights'. For days before Diwali houses will be cleaned, whitewashed and done up for it is firmly believed that the Goddess Lakshmi will come into the cleanest and the best kept houses.

In every section of society and in all age groups the festival is important and for children it is the fireworks, which hold the greatest charm. From the little 'rockets' to the so called 'bombs', all kind of firecrackers are on display and at one point of time I think it was a matter of great pride to spend huge amounts of money on them and also a matter of prestige to buy lots of expensive shinies. The festival supports a huge industry of firecrackers in itself. With the growing awareness of pollution and its attendant negatives amongst the school children now, there is an attempt to reduce the overall display of these 'phatakas' but the revelry is still very colorful, noisy and smoky.

Days after Diwali a cloud of smog will hang over the city and the air will smell of the burnt crackers which will bother everyone with bronchitis or asthma but that is another matter altogether.

I will not be celebrating this year. It is an accepted form of grieving to not celebrate any festival for at least a year. But the season and its merry making do make me feel better even though I am somewhat detached from it. Revelers on the streets, sales and bargains everywhere and gift packs that just seem to get more and more ornate. I remember from my childhood when my grandfather would make these little packets of mixed dry fruits, almonds, cashew nuts, kishmish or the sultanas and chilgoza that is also a dry fruit. These would then be put into small boxes and gift-wrapped. Today we see them all over, packed and ornate. The boxes seem to be getting fancier and fancier with glitter, beads and ribbons and the actual amount of stuff in them actually lesser and lesser.

A mark of the times.

The outside has begun to have so much more meaning that the inside is overlooked. The same could be said of human beings too. It is now so important to wear the right clothes, carry a designer bag, sport a fancy watch and drive the right car that the actual worth of a person may well have very little importance.

Walking down a market street I am looking into the shop windows when it strikes me that I haven't shopped for anything for myself, read clothes and shoes in months. There was a time when this would seem impossible with shoes being bought at the drop of a hat, the answer to so many problems being

"Why don't you go get yourself a new pair of shoes?"

This would invariably make life look better, shopping, spending hours over various items of clothing, mulling over the different colors, designs and often buying very little after spending hours in the mall or the market. I think this strikes Kiya too for I get a call from her saying

"I think we should spend a day together, at the mall. We can have a meal there and you could do with some new clothes. Lets do it. There are lots of sales and we can get some real bargains"

Halfheartedly I agree. Not that I wouldn't like some decent clothes but I know it will trigger off a lot of memories and make me miserable finally.

"Is this how I am going to be for the rest of my life", I think to myself, every little mundane activity reminding me of a togetherness lost. For I always used to shop for clothes with

Diven, needing his approval or doubting my own taste, I'm not sure which. Notorious for a blitzy taste in color I could end up buying all kinds of things, which would appeal to me greatly while in the shops and later would lie, unworn and just wasted. I really don't know why that used to happen.

It still happens actually. I have many explanations amongst the most acceptable to me is the PMS one. As per this theory what happens is that during the PMS phase moods are labile, temperamental and so one naturally looks to shopping as a mood elevator, then, because it is the PMS time, ones tastes and judgment are also altered so one may end up with buys which later lose appeal. Other explanations too can be put forth, the most acceptable one being the fact that marketing and sales is such an art now that the sales persons can convince you that something is looking great on you when it's just the reverse. You figure out the truth later, at home, under husbands critical eye but by then its too late.

So, it may be a good idea, to shop with Kiya. Never can I recall dragging my feet in the manner in which I conducted this shopping expedition, really disinterested and listless. Kiya is great at shopping, her eye discerning and taste good. So I do end up with some good clothes for winter among them a particular esprit jacket in black. They had it in black and in pink, I may have ended up with the pink one had I been on my own but with Kiya one doesn't argue

"What about the pink jacket?" That's me

"Black is classy. Pink is juvenile and what will you wear it with?"

"Can't I wear it with black trousers" still trying to get my
two bits in

"Black makes you look slimmer, always"

"I don't need to look slimmer"

"Black it is, don't argue for the fun of it"

Well, ok, that concluded it and with that we billed for
some other clothes and went on to have some salad, macaroni
and a sweet concoction titled 'Death by chocolate', enjoying
our meal and lingering over our time together, comfortable
and stuffed.

"What are you doing for Diwali?" Kiya asks me

"I am at home" I reply

"Do you think that's a good idea?. Why don't you either
come over to my place or go over to your Dad's? I don't think
you should be on your own."

"I'll be fine Kiya, I've thought about it and I want to be
home"

And not be a wet blanket in everybody's celebrations.
I have thought about it and decided to invite over another
person, not a friend in the true sense of the word, but someone
I like, a colleague, much younger than me, over for dinner.
Sangeeta, who is ever willing and smiling, tells me with no
rancor

"I can come over on Diwali evening, but I will leave early"

What would I do without her, I don't know? Sara, who I
am planning to call over, is to the best of my knowledge, very
much on her own in Delhi with no family. She had been going
through a rough time in her personal life I have been told

by the youngsters, she is going through a particularly messy divorce. Seems like she could do with someone to spend the evening with and so could I.

"Sara, what are you doing on Diwali? Are you on call?"

"No, Ma'am" she replies

"Would you like to spend the evening with me? I am on my own too."

"Sure, Ma'am I would love to"

So that was it. Though the mood wasn't totally happy it wasn't dismal either. Sara and I, working in the same hospital where she is much my junior, do have a great deal in common. We have read the same books and enjoy the same kind of music. It should be a passably pleasant evening I think.

Sangeeta prepares the meal and leaves. We sit around, talking and watching the decorations and the lighting in houses all around us while we sit in the house, which is standing in darkness, so different from the rest. Strangely it doesn't hurt as much as I had thought it would. My mind is slowly calming and maybe accepting. In the house across, the Khanna's place, we can hear much noise and laughter, with children squealing with delight, the crash of a glass falling to the floor and breaking and much scolding and instructions. Their daughter is visiting for Diwali with her two kids and their presence is a pleasant change for my usually quiet neighbors.

Sitting on the verandah with a Sara I try and draw her out and find myself listening to her story. Nothing unusual these days, met a young man and fell in love, married against her parent's wishes. But it's the after that's hurtful because the honeymoon didn't last long. His family created problems apparently and he didn't stand by Sara. A downhill spiral, other women, drinking a lot and beating her up and the marriage was on the rocks. Attempts by her to pacify him or to make a go of the marriage had not worked and they decided to each go their own way.

I listen to her story and wonder. Divorce is a betrayal of the worst sort to my mind. A breach of trust, breaking the dreams and illusions and often the life of a person.

"Oh, that marriage was made in heaven". One hears this phrase and folks are so fond of saying this one too that

"Marriages are made in heaven and broken on earth"

That, I don't think, is true. I don't think any two people are made in perfect accordance with the other and marriages are not made by chance, they are made by a great deal of effort and hard work by both the partners. A lot of loving and caring and bothering and turning a blind eye to some issues, its like watering a plant and being gentle in every way and letting it get enough sun to allow it to grow. Marriage is not a perfect equation in which some people just turn lucky. It takes two to make it work and if one of the two won't try enough it cant work. It could also be true to say that the balance isn't always level, one partner or the other may have the edge at different points of time. But the caring and the compromise must be there. If one person is shouting the other one must shut up or they could end up killing each other or something like that.

And marriage changes, from the first rosy haze of the honeymoon, to the reality and the routine of everyday life.

Changes also, to a family and the responsibilities that go with it. It isn't a glamorous relationship, far from it. And divorce as I see it is a betrayal of those vows. In a country where marriage is supposed to be a tie "for seven lives" the increasing incidence of divorce is distressing. Have we become intolerant, the women, I mean? More aware and more educated and less willing to take the time-tested back seat. Can't figure that one out but as I hear Sara narrate the story of her marriage I feel sad for her. So young and so much heartbreak and I find myself thinking that maybe, in a way, death is kinder. It is something, which you can't fight and the memories are fond and cherished. There is pain but your illusions are not shattered. Grief is very real but you need not regret it. Regrets are hurtful and make you bitter and scar your soul forever.

I hope I was able to help her in a small way to overcome her sadness. We had dinner and since it was late I had her stay over. It was not as bad as I had expected and was in fact rather pleasant.

After Diwali, Delhi gets cold. And cold can be pleasant or it can be raining, chilly and wet. It doesn't snow in Delhi but the temperatures can be very low in December and January touching upto 2 or 3 degrees. Woolens are out and the cold appreciated, by and large, for it is short-lived. Pulling on my coat as I dress to go to work I see my muffler and realize that I haven't walked in so long, more than six months to be precise.

Getting up early in the morning as I am wont to do I find myself often feeling stiff, my back aching and various joints complaining at the effort of movement. As doctors we can be surprisingly pessimistic coming up with the worst possible diagnoses for ones own likely afflictions. Arthritis? I wonder to myself or just aging? Maybe I can speak to someone in the hospital about it. Cafeterias and coffee places in hospitals are places for much light hearted discussion of all aspects of health and disease especially the patients, the diseases, the emergency and the tragedies or the wins.

Hearing doctors talk about death and disease may give a lay person reason to have little faith in the profession for almost everything is made light of, from patients to serious illness and death. Often the hotbeds of hospital gossip too these are areas where people who deal daily with the reality of death and disease let off steam and get a bit of relaxation. Comments like this can abound

"Oh boy, did you hear about Chauhan. He removed the wrong kidney and nobody had a clue. After the surgery the patient didn't pee and so they did an ultrasound. There was no kidney. He had removed the single kidney".

"There were twins and of course the radiologists hadn't picked it up. At the time of the CS she says after delivering the first baby . . .Oh wait, there's another one".

"You wont believe this guy who came to emergency yesterday, holding his ear in his hand. Apparently the dog bit it off".

These somewhat crude and often targeted comments are not meant to hurt or ridicule. Dealing with harsh realities of our profession makes doctors stress bust in these places where so many of us are present who will understand the often hidden emotions behind these seemingly unfunny statements.

The 'Lounge' is the area where the consultant crowd gather for tea, coffee or something cold to drink with some snacks and often the place where you 'pick brains', the informal consultation. So going for coffee in the morning I ask a friend

"DM, Lately I have lots of aches and pains. Need to take a Brufen sometimes"

"Any fever?" DM asks me

"No" I reply

"Joint swelling?" DM continues

"No, no swelling, but my knees often feel stiff in the morning. Better as the day goes on"

"Ok, here's what I'd say. Get a Vitamin D level done. We're all vitamin D deficient these days; it's almost an epidemic. It could be the reason for all these pains. If its normal then we will check further. Do you take any calcium?"

"No I don't. Should I? My diets pretty ok"

"No issue. Get that Vitamin D level and then get back to me".

"Ok, thanks DM"

"I can easily take Vitamin D, why do I need to get levels done?"
I think to myself, and then reminding myself that doctors are often the worst patients I decide to follow his advise.

So I head off to the lab to get my vitamin D levels done. To my disbelief the results come back showing a level of 6ng/ml where the normal value is written as 20 to 40 ng/ml. I am horrified to see this. And I thought I was in good health. Pictures of bone problems, myself with a fractured hip, in a wheelchair or walking with a stick come to my mind and scare me. I will do as he says and I may even get a bone density test done.

When I go back to DM with the test report he tell me
"Take some Vitamin D. And eat some supplemental calcium. And get some exercise. We aren't getting any younger, all of us"

And he goes on to tell me why we are all at risk for Vitamin D deficiency. For as kids we all would play out in the sun but over time and with affluence our exposure to sunlight has lessened considerably. Sedentary lifestyles, a lot of time spent in front of TV and computer screens and much less spent outdoors are the culprits responsible for the present near epidemic of this condition. The industrialization with its attendant pollution and clouds of smog isn't helping either, he tells me.

Suitably chastened, armed with his prescription and so many good intentions I get the Vitamin D and calcium from the chemist. I did take the Vitamin D but the calcium tablets, with their dry and chalky taste were favored only for a few days. After that they gathered dust in my cabinet. But this Vitamin D thing did set me thinking. Not so long in the tooth but getting there. One reads about fractures and the many bone density issues in post menopausal women. But I'm not postmenopausal, I reassure myself. Not that far from it either is the answer my mind gives me. Definitely the bit about exercise is something that needs attention.

And I could certainly do with some exercise, I realize as I pay attention to my reflection in the mirror for a change. Not much weight gained but the flab is evident. I have got a tiny paunch and my once toned arms and legs now appear flabby. And exercise releases endorphins, I tell myself in the mirror. These are the body's "feel good hormones". I could start walking again but it doesn't seem to hold any appeal. The roads are dirty, there is litter everywhere and the only park, which was close to the house, the municipal corporation has dug up for no good reason. The sports club? I ponder, too far and I'd need to drive to get there and the effort would most probably made me give up in no time at all.

"Join a gym"

One of my colleagues advises. She is a trim and fit lady, smart and slim with an athletic body. A regular gymmer, Samaira looks nowhere near her 55 years. Looking at her, older than me after all, I decide that if she can do it so can I.

"Or you could join a Pilates workshop"

"Power Yoga"

"Aerobics I tell you, I can swear by it"

Don't ask for advice if you don't want it. I get so many suggestions that my mind boggles. Where have I been the past few years?

I think over this and decide to go over the various options. It's amazing that once you are aware and looking so many choices appear. While driving home I now begin to pay attention to the signboards and the advertising hoardings on the way. So I find 'Tone up', 'Slim line', 'Get fit' and many such other innovative places. Having no idea what to really expect I decide, in all seriousness to go and pay a visit to one 'Pilates Workshop' and check it out.

Bemused somewhat by the chrome and glass décor I ask the girl at the reception

"May I see the workout once or don't you allow that?"

"Our next session will be beginning at 5 pm Ma'am. You are welcome to watch"

Waiting for the 5 pm session I see all the stuff on display. Vitamin mixes, protein supplements, Aloe Vera juice and some unrecognizable names. And clothes to work out in, tiny shorts and tanks and animal print leotards. Exercise is certainly serious business here. When the session starts I watch from the side. Blaring music and fast movements, lithe, energetic, beautiful toned bodies working out with some balls and some platform which is somewhat elevated and which required them to step up on it and back up and step down. Isn't there anyone here over 25 years of age I ask myself, dismayed as I see them do exercises and moves which could make a contortionist squirm. I can't do that, my knees would never tolerate it, I think to myself, I'll break a bone and then where will I be?

The Gym it will have to be. There is no shortage of gyms either. In the past 2 decades the awareness about physical fitness and the near obsession of the younger generation with working out and having 'hot' bodies has led to a mushrooming of all kind of health related businesses. Gyms, Spas, Fitness centers, you name it and we have them all. Keeping in mind that I really intend to gym I find out about the rates and the available options. A flyer with the newspaper on Sunday announces that the gym in one of the nearby hotels has been done up and they now have an Olympic medal winner as the fitness trainer. Sounds impressive, this is the place. And the fitness trainer bit sounds good. Living close to our apartment is a couple that appear more trendy and fashionable than the rest, driving a fancy car and having a hectic social life. This girl, she had a 'Personal trainer' and would often be seen in the evenings in the small park in the complex doing some workout, with the trainer which whenever I was at a loose end and watching seemed to involve a lot of jumps and high kicks. But the 'Personal trainer' bit sounds organized. And so does this fitness trainer.

The gym is called 'Olympus' and is located in a five star hotel not far from where I live. Walking distance, if you would walk it, and the approach green and clean so that is not a deterrent. The gym itself is located in a part of the hotel, which is sectioned off from the main lobby, and has a separate approach and entrance, as is often the case. Walking into the lobby of this hotel I am pleasantry surprised at the discreetness of the décor and the courtesy of the staff. It is a hotel, which is a bit way out, and I had not expected a very good standard.

Half expecting to see semi clad people on their way to the pool or exercise enthusiasts in leotards I notice a signboard which states very emphatically that no form of informal clothing is allowed in this part of the hotel and that persons on their way to the pool or the gym may use the other entrance specifically provided for that purpose. This settles my unreasonable apprehensions to some extent.

Speaking at the front office and getting directions to the gym, I inquire about the fees for membership and find that they have many kinds of packages which include the saunas, Ayurveda massage therapies, some kind of stone therapies and the gym itself. I am informed that the trainer is an Olympic medal winner, but that I was aware of.

"You would have some forms to fill and some paperwork to complete before you can join", she tells me, this young lady at the reception counter.

"I will come and take the forms from you on my way back after seeing the gym" I tell her as I make my way to the exercise area.

Some pleasing strains of music float up as I climb down the stairs and I can see a number of fancy machines as I walk in. The treadmill, for I am familiar with that one, a lot of weights and presses and some machines for rowing I suppose from the look of it. It is a big place, spacious and airy, and does not seem to be very busy but I could have come at the wrong time of the day. There are some sections of the gym, which are marked male and female designating the shower and sauna areas I guess.

A smart and not so young man walks up to me.

"Good afternoon. May I help you?"
"I just wanted to see the gym. I am planning to join"
"I am Amir, he introduces himself. The trainer"
I give him no introduction of my self and ask instead
"Can you tell me something about working out, what kind of exercises one should do to start and what are the risks of sustaining injury for persons who are not used to working out?"

He looks me over in a somewhat clinical fashion and I squirm inwardly. What am I hoping for? That someone should say

"Oh you look very fit. You hardly look as though you need to join a gym"

Oh, our fantasies.

Far from it

"Well we all have problems in the waist area with age and you" . . . . Inspecting me from head to toe he continues "this part you know", putting his hands on his thighs, "the Indian figure is a bit heavy there isn't it?" and then goes on to explain a bit about the basics of starting an exercise programme, the cardio workouts and the dietary amendments.

"Oh boy, we aren't very diplomatic are we", I think, but for once I am so committed to this idea that I do not take offense at his statements. Like a schoolteacher encouraging her wards to do better I tell myself and so feeling somewhat intimidated still I make my way up to the reception area again.

The pretty miss at the reception asks me
"Well, Ma'am how did you like our gym?"
"Impressive" I reply with a smile and she goes on
"Should I give you the forms to fill?"
"Yes"

I take the forms and seat myself at one of the tables in the lobby itself and start filling them. Name, age, gender, work, address, I fill it out diligently till I come to Marital status. What business is it of theirs? I think, starting to get upset, and the choices are single and married. How illogical is that and so archaic.

Why couldn't they have been like Facebook where you have so many choices like 'Its complicated' and 'In a relationship' not that I was but still.

Am I single? I guess that's how it is but my mind refuses to accept that tag. If I'm supposed to fill out this form I better get on with it.

"I don't have my glasses and I can't read very well without them", I say to the girl at the reception

"I will fill it out at home and come back with it tomorrow"

I never went back to that hotel or that gym.

Searching For 'Me'

"I seem to have lost myself
In the walks of life
I really need to find for me,
A small dose of magic"

I have realized over the past few months that I am lost. Not lost as in wandering in the jungle but lost as in the 'I' was lost. In the past nearly twenty years everything I thought or planned was for a 'We'. Now there is no we there's just an I. And I no longer know how to think as an 'I'. I try to recall myself as what I was before all this happened and find that though I was a realist I was also a romantic and a bit of a dreamer. Faith in life, faith in God and faith that nothing can really go wrong. Life can be meaningless without faith.

When Diven was diagnosed with cancer I thought
"This cannot happen. It will be all right. God cannot be so unkind, he cannot be so cruel to us"
But he was, life was cruel, snatching away from me the biggest magic of my life, my sweetheart.
I used to believe, believe in the good things in life, and believe in magic.

Magic exists you know. It's all around us, we just don't see it. It's there in the toothless beaming smile of a baby, in the dance of the peacock showing off its plumage as the skies turn overcast, it's there in the smell of the wet earth after the first shower of the monsoon. There's magic in the hand your mother puts on your brow when you are not well and it's there when you hug your friend when she's upset.

But the heart grieves and the mind turns jaded and we just don't see it anymore. It's for me now to look for magic in life for life without some magic is meaningless, an existence and not living.

There are so many things that defy logic and reason but we still refuse to completely disbelieve or firmly reject. Dreaming of the impossible at some point or the other has led to the major discoveries and inventions. The human mind is the most amazing of all machines. Where we may come apart at the seams for trivial things we can sometimes find strength to sustain the spirit when all is lost. It's easy to dream and especially when reality seems hard to face. I spent many an evening imagining different lifestyles for myself from living in a cottage in the mountains with a spring flowing in the garden, far removed from the big city, cool, peaceful, green and far away from human habitation to an island in the Bahamas.

Maybe a remote destination in the Himalayas.

All manner of bizarre thoughts seemed to find place in my mind. I read about rebirth, reincarnation and subsequent lives. This is obviously a much-researched topic and holds intense fascination for so many, so much written on topic that facts and fiction merge. There was at this time a television show with a specialist in taking you to your past lives to decipher how you came to have certain phobias, or became a part of certain events.

The psychiatrists will take everything to our childhood to sort out our problems and this will take us even further, to past lives. All this holds immense appeal at certain times in our lives, the times when reality hurts and when it's nice to believe in magic. A kind of escapism.

I take to finding things to amuse myself and as usual ask for advice . . . will I never learn?

"Join a singles group. You know singles who go out for movies together, or plays or dinner"

"Join a satsang" A satsang is a religious group and meet for discourses

"Take up a musical instrument"

All well meaning suggestions but nothing appeals.

Even good memories are a kind of magic. You can go back to them and relive them and no one can take them away from you, ever. I live in my memories. It's easier that way sometimes. Haven't eaten out in so long, haven't called for pizza, haven't gone for a movie or a play. Starts a train of thought, of memories, some good, and some silly. Pizza memories.

It's not unusual in India to have full time servants and doesn't necessarily denote affluence. If you have enough space to keep another person, preferably outside of your own living space, you can have full time help. And till very recently, actually not so very recently but till a year or so before my husband's illness we had always had one. The last one, a young man Hansraj, had spent a long time with us. Coming to live with us at around 17 years of age, he was with us for 8 years, so over the years was a part of the family knowing our eating and wearing preferences, familiar with family and friends and generally over a period of time more a part of our world than his own.

He would take a month off in the year and go to his village and visit his family who are farmers. His village being a fair distance meant he travelled for nearly two days to get there and two days to get back and so he often wanted more than a month off or landed back after 5 weeks instead of four. The point is, one gets so used to help in the house, that when you have to do even simple tasks, it palls. The month without Hansraj would mean my workload would double, both home and the workplace. Since we were often just the two of us it wasn't really difficult. My cooking, however, is nothing to write home about, basic and serving its purpose. I can put together a fair meal and do enjoy some exotic recipes but doing it on an everyday basis gets irritating.

So it would invariably mean that by the time our fellow was due back I'd be nearing the end of my tether.

And often it would mean my saying to Diven
"Not in a mood to cook tonight, Lets call for pizza"
Mind you he loves pizza whichever way it comes, hot or cold, fresh or yesterdays. Said he thought it was great how

Sylvester Stallone cut his pizza with a scissor in some movie. But ask to call for pizza when Hansraj is not there and the answer is invariably

"No, I don't want pizza. You make something"

"Baby, I'm tired and don't want to cook" I repeat myself. I may as well be talking to the wall

"Cook something simple, just rice and dal. I'll do the dishes"

He'd win and he'd do the dishes. But this isn't the issue here.

Two days later

Hansraj back, thank the Lord, and one is back to being pampered and the 'Memsahib'. Getting chicken legs from the market and explaining to him how we are going to do them, marinate them, cook them

Diven says

"I am going to call for pizza".

"But he's here, he'll cook" I say, completely flummoxed and a bit irritated too, and mind you Hansraj was a good cook, far better than me. Arguments don't work.

"I'm calling for it. Even Hansraj loves pizza"??

Pizza he wants so pizza we get.

I could never understand this but it happened year after year and I figured that for some reason he either likes my cooking or likes being waited on and I still don't know.

When Diven became unwell, we were unaware of the gravity of the situation. His voice became hoarse and somewhat rough. He was a smoker and everyone thought he had laryngitis. He didn't.

As his disease progressed his voice became softer and the treatment, the radiation therapy, initially made it worse. I was able to hear him easily even when he spoke in a hoarse whisper, but at that point he was painfully conscious of it. Being at home during this time he often ate and enjoyed his pizzas. That was until the radiation blasted his taste buds. He had a hard time speaking on the phone so he'd call me at work or text me

"Dominoes, Farm fresh pizza double, with extra cheese and two bbq chicken wings"

I would text back an "Ok" and then call Dominoes and order telling him "Done" and getting a smiley in answer.

So for old times sake I decide to call for pizza. I call Dominoes and order

"Farm fresh pizza, single and one chicken bbq wings"

"Your number, Ma'am?" the voice at the other end

What's wrong, don't they have caller identity? I give my number

"Ok, Mr. Diven" I get a cheerful reply. Moron I think, do I sound like Mr. Diven, or a Mr. anything for that matter. Retard.

"Please change that to Ms. Anita please"

And that's that.

I have to move. Move as in change house. Go live elsewhere. Find a new place. Leave here where we lived together for so many years. Panicking at the implications and trying to figure out how I am going to do it. It has it good points I tell myself. May be good to leave this house where there are so many memories attached to every little thing. Make a fresh start. The chain of events leading to this is distressing but surprisingly don't cause me as much trauma as I might have anticipated. It's just a house after all.

Why are we married to brick and mortar? We give so much importance to such things that the really important things become secondary. I decide at some point that with him gone in any case the house doesn't have much meaning. Yes there are memories but the memories I will carry with me so what do I care. The practicalities bother me I have no idea where to start, the estate agent, the brokers or just word of mouth. I will have to take time off from work and pack up. A lot of the furniture has been in the house ever since we moved in, five years ago and so I can easily get rid of it. Maybe a fresh start will help.

It wasn't easy finding a new place but it wasn't difficult moving. Much simpler than I thought it would be in fact. I went and saw flats and high rises, not the really high ones but tall enough like cubbyholes and the lifts make me claustrophobic and so I didn't like any of them. They are decidedly more secure but don't appeal. Finally found an area with houses divided into three flats each, pretty tree lined avenues and plenty of parking space. Parking space is very important in Delhi; you can get killed in fights over it. Somebody recently did get killed, I read in the papers, so a good parking space is a plus.

A ground floor flat, some space at the back with a toilet presumably meant for a servant and an area in front, small, cant be called a garden it has a small paved space and then a small area which has some plants. It has a 'Tulsi' plant growing there and some azaleas and I finally decide on it. The Tulsi or the Basil leaves are considered auspicious in India and even revered and they have medicinal properties.

Maybe it's an omen, well, I hope.

I had already decided that when I pack house I will give away some of his clothes. Not all. His favorite things will stay with me and some of his old tee shirts I wear when I sleep. They are way too big for me but they make me feel better. Inspite of my decision when I actually sit down with his clothes it hurts so much I can hardly breathe. Every article of clothing brings with it memories and I hide my face in his clothes and cry. The blue Levis denim jacket, well worn, such a favorite and the camouflage pants which he often wore when we went for the radiation therapy. We'd go for the radiation early so he'd be the first patient and wouldn't have to meet too many people.

"You can easily go in tracks", I told him

"No, I cant. You work there. People will notice"

So every morning he'd dress well to go for the radiation therapy. Full sleeved shirt and trousers.

And a handkerchief.

He was the only man I can think of who always carried a hanky, folks don't often these days. Handkerchiefs were bought with the same attention that some men give to buying their ties and he ironed them himself. Nobody else could get it right.

"Oh baby stay with me" I think and *"lets go to the new house. I'm so tired sometimes of doing everything myself, stay with me"*

I often still conduct these conversations with him. I feel he listens wherever he is and I get strength from the thought.

Call it what you will.

I watch the priest conducting the 'Pooja' in the new house as we sit on the floor for moving into a new place too has its set rituals. This 'Panditji' or priest doesn't look old enough to even shave I'm thinking to myself as he recites the prayers in Sanskrit and the heat from the small fire he has lit gives off smoke and makes me cough. First 'Pooja' in my entire life which I have sat alone for. I focus on other practical issues, neat and freshly whitewashed house will have smoke darkening the ceiling and walls even before I have moved in I think and I will plant some flowers. It's ok. I'll survive.

Sitting behind me is Sangeeta, my maid, who has made the necessary arrangements. The house is nearly empty of furniture having only a desk of walnut wood and a decorative chest of drawers. Not much to show for so many years of marriage. The kitchen is however complete with china, crystal, dinner sets and all kind of gadgets. Too tired to worry about all this I have brought over a bed, which was lying in the storage basement, to sleep on and will manage the rest later. My stuff is in the cartons in the living room.

The sheer physical exhaustion of packing and sorting out my belongings has exhausted me. I sleep well contrary to what I had expected. Maybe I am fanciful but houses have a feel to them and this house has a happy feel. Where we had lived earlier was a place I had never wanted to live in. I was convinced even before we went there that it was 'inauspicious' but these are feelings which no one pays heed to in the practical doings. But all the same I am reassured because my new house has a 'good' feel.

Shopping for furniture wasn't tough. I go with Kiya and everything I like, she disagrees with, too big, too small, too impractical, our usual sparring continuing. I love shopping with her or I'd end up with pink sofas and fluorescent curtains. I enjoy having her behave as though she's my mom I think and

"Black leather sofa? Why would you want that?"

"It's looking very nice", I say

"That's here because there is so much space, the showroom is so large. Your living room isn't so big so it will dwarf it and black gets dirty"

Finally we decide on a rather pretty pale fawn color which we both like but I can also see is a bit fanciful and leather needs care

"Its pale, will get dirty easily. You don't have kids so that's a good thing. Sure you want leather?"

"Yes"

So that's done. I get a bed for myself and leave the rest to be done bit by bit as time goes on.

What's my hurry?

No hurry and that shows for even weeks later some of the cartons are still lying packed and in the other bedroom.

By bed I don't mean a single. No my home is a house is done like a home for two. It's big enough in any case and it's a habit that's difficult to change had I even wanted to do so at this time. A nice double bed and side tables and the second bedroom to be done at leisure and when the finances permit. Gave away some of his clothes but some things cannot be given away.

The little things, which were so much his. The manicure sets, the knives, not all functional like the Swiss knives which I have practically every kind of, the one with twenty attachments and the thinner one, the one that goes on a key ring and the one which has a sign of zodiac on it and even a Swiss card knife but also pretty, decorative knives. A compass, silver souvenirs from various countries and some badges. And the lovely plates of that bluey material, Wedgewood and the silver Sheffield curios.

And some of the other little artifacts. We have momentos from most of the places we visited from the ashtray form the hotel in which we spent our honeymoon to some airline spoons. Nowadays the entire cutlery is plastic but there was a time when it was stainless steel. So I have spoons, which say 'IA' and also an ashtray from an armrest in the flight.

Sometimes it could be positively embarrassing the way he'd pick things. Having dinner at a really fancy restaurant one night he says to me

"Watch that bag of yours. Its got stuff"

Knowing what he is capable of I freak out seeing myself being checked by security and then washing dishes in the hotel. Giving him a dirty look

"What is it and for Gods sake, why my bag? If you want to do these silly kleptomaniacal activities at least have the decency to put the stuff in your own pockets".

"Well your bag is so big and has so much junk in it that a little bit more won't even be noticeable"

Fuming, I sweat it out for the rest of the meal, itching to get it over and see what he has put in it and not daring to even go to the restroom to check. What if they have cameras there?

When we leave and only once we are safely in our own car do I dare to look and what do I have? Pretty and silly cocktail shakers one like an ostrich, another a giraffe and one like a long necked don't know what bird. Pretty but silly. How can I give or throw any of these away?

All go into the side table on the other side of the bed. At that time I was actually obsessed with having a place, which he could come back to anytime, had that been likely to happen. We need our dreams and we need the magic. Some of his clothes, more expensive and fancy still stayed in the closet with mine. And the golf sets which I don't wish to give away ever. It's not obsessive or denial or anything like that as the shrinks would love to say, it's just that its not possible to let go of everything at one time, all at once.

Bedroom set up, the air-conditioning, inverter for back up of electricity all had to be sorted out. At the end of it all I am actually quite pleased with myself for having managed it to my satisfaction. It may not have been an Olympian task but for me it was an achievement. But after the sheer adrenaline drive of moving waned off the sadness tends to set in, the awareness that he is not here to share all this with and that now finally having left the old house I seem to have severed all ties.

Kiya comes over to inspect the house and stays for hours. She likes it here and thinks that it will be good for me

"Don't brood, think of happy things"

"Yes, I am positive, it feels good"

Later, the evening is quiet and peaceful and, I stand at the window looking out. The night is starry and I can see people walking outside, some kids with bicycles and some delivery boy whistling cheerfully as he rings a bell. I walk and have always walked in the morning. Looking outside I wish I could walk now, late at night but habits of a lifetime run deep and I am scared. Thinking to myself

If, if I had a dog maybe I could take him for a walk.

A nice big dog, which would be enough to scare a potential robber or whatever.

For incidents of chain snatching and robbery are commonplace in Delhi. If you are going to be walking on the roads in Delhi it would not be advisable to wear jewelry or basically gold. Gold tempts robbers and there are incidents when boys or men approach on a motorcycle and snatch at the ornaments or even show knives. Has happened in broad daylight and in the best of residential colonies.

So, if I had a dog, I muse then . . . Then I could walk at night

An idea has seeded itself in my brain and though initially very half-baked I start to give it serious thought. I live alone and it wont is easy. A big dog or a small dog? And who would look after it the whole long day while I am at work? Still the thought works like a worm in my brain and I decide to research it some more.

As a child I did not grow up in Delhi. I grew up in a small town in the hills, green and verdant. Big houses and gardens, which you cant dream of in Delhi. The valley of Kashmir has been called a 'Paradise on earth' for its natural beauty. Growing up we always had dogs in the house; only at that time they were my mothers dogs. I don't recall ever training a dog or doing any of the dirty work. That was my mom's domain. We, my brother and I, we just enjoyed them. Walked them sometimes or showed them off if they were worth it. In my husbands family the 'pet' concept didn't exist. There are actually two kinds of people in the world, they are the 'dog people' and there are the 'no dog people'. And though initially I was keen it got suggested out of my mind for no one wanted a dog there. You have to love dogs, or else what would be the point keeping one.

Dogs apart, we've had all kinds of pets as children. A cat, which isn't really a very affectionate pet, turtles, who tend to die rather easily and even a monkey. The monkey we got by default. This little monkey got separated from its mother and was brought to our house by someone in the hope that we would keep it. We did. It was mischievous and very temperamental. But there in Kashmir there was lots of space and it was really no hardship keeping it though she had to be tied up when she was in one of her moods. Monkeys are very like humans and can mimic our actions with accuracy. Can peel bananas, drink from a glass and eat with a spoon. And the dogs they were invariably free to wander in and out of the house.

If I get one here how will I manage it?

The first thing I need to sort out is what breed of dog. Big, or small. That's tough, but for me, I like the bigger dogs. Kiya has dog, a Chihuahua and I don't like it very much, and it's yappy and practically hairless and looks like a large and worried rat. Small dogs tend to be ill tempered more often than not and, I think they are, like, insecure. Anyone can kick them or step on them. And they have a very high-pitched bark. Also they are relatively fragile, if they get unwell, you can lose them very easily. My heart quails. No, a small dog is out.

So then, a big dog. Not so many options there for there's only a few you could keep in a house and so little space. Can you imagine a St Bernard in one of these piddly flats? No, out. Even the German Shepherds are big dogs though I have seen one in the neighborhood. Thinking dogs, I start noticing the ones around when I go for my walk in the morning. They're a few beautiful ones around, golden dogs with long floppy ears and lots of hair, the cocker spaniels. And the dotty, spotty, black and white one, those are the Dalmatians. And the beautiful white, fluffy ones the Pekinese or the Lhasa apsos.

But the ones I like are the Labs. The Labradors. White, or golden or black. Often fat. And very friendly. They don't snap at you and the one I see being walked by its owner seems placid and slow.

Suits me.

I am going to go and see some Labrador puppies. If you don't want to keep a dog, never go and see puppies. No matter what the dog is finally going to look like puppies are all beautiful and very appealing. I check on the net and ask around me. No harm in going to have a look and if I don't want to buy I needn't I tell myself in all seriousness.

It's June in Delhi the hottest month in the year. Its better than winter to get a dog, at least the washing and cleaning will not be so difficult. My mind is already slowly bringing a dog into my life. If I have to give up this idea it's going to hurt.

I gingerly approach the topic to Sangeeta, my maid. After all keeping a dog is messy and it will increase her workload. I am prepared to argue my point with her and also to pay her more for she will also have to pitch in to look after the animal. If she hates dogs it's going to be a bit difficult.

I am amused at my line of thought, *"Who is employed by whom?"* But she is pleasant and reliable and so far has not given my any reason for complaint. I do not wish to find myself in a kind of standoff.

But I am pleasantly surprised. Sangeeta is delighted with the idea.

"That will be very nice for you, she says. Its good to have a dog in the house"

"Its also a lot of hard work"

"That is fine"

"Messy"

"Aap le aayo" You get it. "It will be ok"

This dog has taken on an identity in my mind now. A male dog or a bitch?

Will decide when I go to see.

And a name. What do I name my doggie?

Dogs are named on all kind of fancies. Someone I know their dogs always had roman names like Ceaser, Brutus. And another lot the names of drinks like Brandy and Cocoa.
Oh well a lot of scope for imagination.

Merlin was a sorcerer in the sixteenth century. It is said that he engineered the birth of King Arthur. Whether he really existed or was a myth is a moot point but he was a powerful wizard and he was a friend, philosopher, advisor and guide to King Arthur. Possibly his creator was inspired by Myrrdin who was a prophet and bard in the ninth century and Ambrosius, a chronicler. It is said that Merlin did not have a mortal father but was begot by a mortal woman and an incubus.

Whatever. Merlin was powerful magic and I could do with some magic in my life. My dog will be called Merlin.

June is ending by the time I finally decide on going to go and see puppies. The monsoon is generally expected in Delhi in the last week of June but it is invariably delayed. Trust my luck this time it on time. Mr. Gaurav, who I had contacted on the net and who had told me they have a litter of Labrador puppies and he will call me when they are ready to be separated from their mother. He doesn't speak very good English and changes his number every time he calls. Not a very reliable source for a dog I am convinced. Then I wont buy it.

The point is when you see the puppies you have to be well versed with dogs to recognize a pedigreed one. Puppies are all pretty and apart from the color and the hair on them a little difficult to recognize. Could judge by the snout I think and by this or that. Back again to fretting for no rhyme or reason.

Are there times when we are guided? I wouldn't have been a great one for relying on that one but for this one time I will say I was. I am not sure what led me to make up my mind but

It s the middle of a working day, I get a call from Mr. Gaurav saying

"You can come and see the puppies today, Madam"

Ordinarily this would have got my back up. Today?? Cant you give a person choices like today or tomorrow

"Today or tomorrow?" I ask him. It's pouring

"Today" he replies firmly

Very shady character I think, I will go and see and say no.

As I leave hospital, having told my colleagues that I have something important come up suddenly and on the way I text my colleague

"Going to see a dog. A puppy"

He texts back "Why just see. Get it"

For some reason that did it. I will get the dog. If this fellow is shady, like I keep on feeling all that can happen is that he will sell me a dog, which is not a pedigreed one, and make money. What else can happen? Nothing more calamitous.

Worse come to worse I will land myself with a mongrel. And suddenly it no longer matters. A dog is a dog at the end of the day. And mongrels are as faithful and loving as any other. Whichever dog you keep it is finally your dog.

Sheets of rain come down making visibility poor and driving difficult. The 'Monsoon' has finally hit Delhi with a vengeance and what happens to Delhi when it pours is best left unsaid. Waterlogging, traffic jams, electricity failures and total chaos. This is our capital city and so disorganized. Being driven to my destination, which is in some obscure area in the outskirts of Delhi, I am a bit amazed at myself. Traffic is crazy; I have no idea who I am dealing with and no idea what to do with a dog once I get it. And yet I am feeling after so long a feeling of anticipation and pleasure.

We are supposed to meet up in a market place for he says that the place where the puppies are in a bit out of the main town on a kind of farm. So if they are professionals and breeders, we could be fine. When we reach there is no sign of anyone at the assigned crossing and so I call him

"Mr. Gaurav, I am here"

In about two minutes there is a tap at my window. On a motorcycle is a young man, about twenty-five or so and wearing a raincoat. Doesn't look like a criminal

"Follow me, he says"

So we follow till we are out of the main marketplace and on a kind of side road. He stops and says

"Please wait here, I'll get the puppies"

??? I think on the road, are they stolen or what. "Ok, I'll wait"

He is back in five minutes and now there are two of them on the bike, his pillion rider about sixteen and carrying a basket. He brings the basket to me and I take it in the car.

"There are three puppies, two male and one female. Labs, like you wanted. They are one month old and healthy. You choose"

I lift the lid of the basket and lift them out, one by one. One black, one tawny and one white with a tinge of gold on his ears.

"Will they stay this color as they get bigger?" I ask

"Yes, may change a little but for most part the color is like this. If you want to see the mother I can take you, but the roads are bad"

"No, its ok" In for a penny, may as well be in for a pound I think

Trying to sound as though I know what I am doing I ask him

"Do they have chips? And what about the papers?"

I am aware that these days they put some computer chips on dogs, especially the very expensive ones I guess, so they may be traced if they are lost or stolen. I don't know anything more than that.

"They are very small. Chips are put later"

By now I have figured out that this is a kind of amateurish dealing but I like the look of the pups. The color is right and the heads are broad and the nose too. They do have lab lineage and but how pedigreed is doubtful.

I reach down and pick them up, one by one.

As I try to pick up the white one he topples over. Picking him up gently, I put him on the car seat beside me and hold his head in my hand. He promptly falls down again. I pick him up and hold him on my lap with his head in the palm of my hand as I try to see his eyes. He just shuts his eyes and flops down, fast asleep.

That's all it took.
I fell in love.

MERLIN

*"You fall in love at first sight
or you don't fall in love at all"*

That's how it started. My story with Merlin. I have got him now. The deed is done. I look at this tiny puppy sleeping on my lap and wonder what exactly I have got myself into. I want the dog but don't know much about the practical aspects of keeping a dog.

I had asked the few preliminary questions before taking the dog from that fellow like how often he needs to be fed and what is he to be fed, but his answers leave me dissatisfied. We'll have to find out for ourselves. But I don't even have any basics.

Driving back I give Sangeeta a call and tell her I've got a puppy and that she had better come in early so we can sort it out and also make up my mind to take the next day off so I can shop for him.

Need to make a list of the things he needs.

Need to find out about doggy food.

Need to find a vet nearby for his shots and routine care.

What about the toilet training?

It's going to be really messy.

The house is going to turn topsy turvy.

It's a nice feeling, though, this little furry baby dog sleeping in my lap and I lift him and cuddle him, loving the soft fur and tiny body. I hope he doesn't pee in the car, on my lap. But he is good, sleeping comfortably and opening his eyes only when I put him down on the floor after I get home.

Sangeeta is waiting and on seeing him she says

"Oh he is so beautiful, 'sundar hai', this dog. He is a labradog isn't he?"

She calls him a labradog and I try to correct her

"Labrador" I say

"Haan, Labradog"

From then to now no amount of correcting has changed that and to date he is a labra dog for her.

Having got the dog there's so much that will need to be sorted and we busy ourselves with the practical aspects. A bowl to feed him some milk and for water for a start. The puppy Merlin is now wandering around the room as though inspecting his new surroundings. So we give him a bowl of milk.

"What if he does not know how to drink from this? He must have been with his mother and breast-feeding" I ask Sangeeta "What then?"

But no such issues. He laps up the milk and promptly before we can do anything there is a small puddle on the floor.

That was the start of things to come, puddles and pee and the mess of a puppy in the house.

"Every time he is fed, we have to take him out immediately" I am trying to sort all this out and lay down some ground rules. I am saying 'we' but for most part I will be doing all this.

Sangeeta picks him up and we take him outside, for after drinking his milk his belly is so full that it protrudes like that of a lady in the late stages of pregnancy.

We both laugh, he looks so funny and he can hardly walk, he totters a little and then sits down again.

This kind of set a precedent and worked to toilet train him. Every time he was fed, within a few minutes I would take him out, to the enclosed area in front of the house and wait till he did his pee or poop whatever. He was so tiny that taking him out on the road was not an option initially and even if it was I was too scared to do it. Later when he was bigger and I had to train him to do it outside, in the open grounds, it was an issue. But for now it was ok, doable.

I took an old cushion and put it on the floor, as I don't have a bed for him. Its warm and he will be fine on the floor but how long will he sleep and will he pee again in the night? Puppies must be feeling some sense of loss when separated from their mothers but our baby seemed happy enough snoozing on the floor half on the cushion and half off it.

I work in a Pediatric ward and so I have some kiddie stuff lying around. There is a small teddy bear about six odd inches high, which is a part of the package we give to kids in the ward on their birthdays or children's day or a festival. I took this teddy and put it next to Merlin. He paid scant attention to my ministrations but over the next few days he would form the habit of sleeping with his head near the tiny bear. He never chewed this up, which could not be said for anything else.

Dog babies too have their own whimsical notions.

I have put him on the floor in my bedroom for I need to keep an eye on him and don't want to leave him alone in the living room. I like having him there I think as I watch him sleep that first night. It feels good though I need to work out so many things.

By this time I was so tired that my eyes were closing of their own accord and I realize I have had enough excitement for one day. Apprehensive that I may step on him if he wanders in the night I keep a night lamp on in the room. As I lie down to sleep I can see him on the floor.

I am no longer alone.

The thought comes to me, a feeling after so long of having company in the night when I am lying down in bed, I feel a sense of calm and its like a tiny ray of sunshine had suddenly touched a dark room. My life most likely.

I fell off to sleep immediately. Waking up, my first thought is Merlin. I have woken up at 5am and there he is, wandering around the room, sniffing. Small and white, fluffy and rounded, with his floppy ears and long somewhat ungainly tail. He is walking and then he sits down and attempts to scratch his ear. Then he squats down and pees. I jump out of bed but it's too late.

There are already two puddles in the room. I get up and my first job is to take him outside again. He will have to be trained slowly. I will clean up the mess after that.

Merlin didn't whine or cry as a tiny puppy. He learned all those tricks and bad habits later when he was nearly a year old. Or maybe when he was that small I was initially so panicky and over active that I never did sleep beyond 5 am and so took him out very early every day.

In the morning I give him some milk again and then sit down to write a list of all the things I am going to need to buy and to do.

Everyone I spoke to seemed convinced that I would not be able to do justice to bringing up a dog with my work schedule but I was convinced that I would be able to manage it for animals tend to settle into whatever routines they are taught. Much like human beings actually that. I heard

"A bit unfair I think, you'll leave the animal for such long hours"

"He will be lonely. Labs tend to get lonely"

"He will turn destructive"

I had turned a deaf ear to all these snippets of information imparted to me in the form of conversation and decide I am going to do it even if I have to employ a sitter for the dog later. That may sound crazy but it can be done too can't it. Well it never came to that but it's just that once I make up my mind I stick by my decisions, come what may. It's the making up of the mind which is difficult, not the after.

I have a long, long list. And so I go shopping for Merlin.

Shopping for Merlin is something I can do on my own, don't need anyone to advise me regarding color and cut for he is unlikely to complain about what I get. That sounds like fun. So I go and get rather carried away. Delhi has so many market places and now the malls that one is spoilt for choice. Going over in my mind the mall I had visited with Kiya when we last went shopping I can't recall seeing any pet shop there. So I go to Khan Market. Khan market is one of the oldest markets in Delhi and it used to be a favorite haunt of ours at one point of time for anything from a meal out to shopping for eatables and exotic fruits and vegetables. You can get anything there, literally as far as food goes certainly for a large fraction of the European and non-Indian crowd shops there. It is considered a relatively expensive and upmarket shopping place. Delhi has some very peculiar and snobbish notions about certain things and this is certainly one of them. But it does have more pet shops than any other market in Delhi that I am aware of.

I go to a store called 'Jaws and Paws' and am totally overwhelmed by the choices, as I don't know what all I am going to need. I think the staff there is quite used to seeing ignorant first time owners of pets for the gentleman there sorting out his accounts after seeing me helplessly gazing at the shelves and sorting out the cat stuff from the dog stuff asks me politely

"Dog or cat, ma'am?"

"Dog" I reply

"How old?"

"Four weeks"

"What breed?"

"A lab" that's me, feeling very pleased. You'd think I had given birth to the dog rather than bought him

"I got him yesterday. He is a male, White"

So he helps me get what I need. Leaving after paying a rather hefty sum I have two bowls, one for milk or food and one for water, two collars, a small leash, a bed, dog 'cerelac', whatever that is, some spray that deters them from peeing there and a spray preventing them from chewing stuff presumably and I am not done as yet. In addition to stuff for him, I need stuff for me too, starting from Dettol to Phenyl to the floor swabbing cloths and gloves. I am only able to get sterile gloves at the chemist, which I don't really need and they are expensive and I note that I should get the unsterile gloves from hospital, which we get in packs of 100s and they are cheap.

Gathering all my shopping I head home and realize that in the past two days I haven't once thought of Diven and cried my eyes out. Though I am pleased with the fact that I am not crying I feel guilty because he has been missing from my thoughts for so long. Is that what is going to happen to me with time, I wonder, the thoughts will become less frequent and that well loved face which I can easily visualize in my minds eye will fade and become more fuzzy? No, that cannot happen and when I get home I pick his photograph from my bedside and look at it for a long time as though I wish to imprint the image in my mind.

Grief is very cunning, and sly as a fox, you start to feel that you are managing to push it behind you when it will suddenly pick its head up and attack you again, leaving you in pieces.

Granted that in time you learn to deal with it, the intensity of the pain becomes less and bearable but it leaves a mark on you which can never be wiped out, it can only be tolerated, lived with and with time hopefully, accepted

I pick up Merlin in my arms and introduce him to Diven

"See baby this is Merlin, he has come to stay with me, to keep me company"

I think he kind of smiled. Actually this is a beautiful picture of my husband, taken by my Dad and wherever I stand in the room he seems to look at me and though he is not exactly smiling, at a certain angle he seems to be in a good mood.

I have two collars for Merlin, its time to put one on. Of the two one is a real collar of leather, pinkish with some stones studded in it, very girlie and the other is a kind of thick ribbon, red, with a tiny jingle on it. The fellow in the pet shop told me that if you don't put a collar on them when they are really tiny they would not be able to get used to it at a later stage. This little red shiny ribbon with its small jingle looks very pleasing on the white fur of the puppy and as he moves around the room the jingle of his collar provides a pleasing musical tinkling sound.

As I get used to having him around, my subconscious mind learns to track the sound of that jingle so that when we shifted him to a proper dog collar I missed it.

My mind working on many different levels I then proceed to unpack a carton, which is filled photographs and the wall decorations of my house. The house is Spartan in its look and I put up some photographs, of him, of him and me, of my mom and brother and of various family gatherings. It is customary in India to put garlands on photographs of people who are no longer in this world. These garlands are usually made of dried roses and shavings of sandalwood or 'Chandan' as it is called. Often in shops or even medical establishments there will be photographs or painted portraits of people with these garlands and you are to pay your respects. Incense may often be lit in front of these pictures, at the start of the day or some important work, a kind of reverence. It is a way of remembering and commemorating our departed loved ones or ancestors.

I find that I am not willing to put any such garland on Diven's pictures. Do I need to make a declaration? The thought is repugnant.

I really do not know why so many or our customs do not appeal to me. I am not a rebel, in fact very much a conformist. Possibly every act that pushes it in my face that he is no longer with me is to be ignored, denied and evaded.

There are so many photographs of us together it will mean putting a garland on myself too, I justify my stance in this denial to conform to the custom. Looking down at my left hand I see the ring I wear on my third finger. A slim gold band, which has been there since the day, it was put on, nearly twenty-one years ago, on my wedding day. I wonder if this is also supposed to be taken off for in our country the usual ornamentation for denoting a married state like the black and gold beaded necklace, the 'Mangal sutra' is to be removed if the husband is no longer alive. The same goes for the vermillion mark on the forehead, the 'sindoor' or the 'toe rings' for all these denote a wedded state.

A wedding band or a gold ring is not an indicator of the married status in our country or at least it used not to be. It was just another piece of jewelry. It's a bit different now. Over the two decades it is now more common to see wedding bands and such like, though it is not a part of our wedding ceremonies.

Our rings, they were incorporated in our wedding ceremony at the request of my husband and he put that ring on my finger just prior to putting the 'mangal sutra' around my neck. It was an unusual and pleasing request for that time. The 'Panditji' had seen no reason to not accede to the unusual plea for it did not interfere with his ceremony in any way. Our wedding ceremonies are long and complicated and conducted in Sanskrit, a language which most of us do not understand and at the end the Panditji gives us his interpretation in Hindi. I feel we may do better with a simple "till death do us part" ceremony in keeping with the times.

I shall not let death part us I think to myself as I look at this simple ring adorning my finger, for he shall live in my heart and my mind, and I keep if firmly on.

But for now Merlin and I, we need to form some kind of a routine for I will be working everyday. Medicine is a demanding profession both physically and mentally. I often work seven days a week and have a longish day on occasion. So I plan my dog's day according to his needs and my convenience.

I feed him in the morning before I leave. And since he is small, I come back at around two, making that extra trip just to feed him and take him out and go back to work again returning finally at around 5.30 or 6 pm.

Gets a bit hectic but when he grows it will be easier.

Many a day on coming in at 2 or 2.30 in the afternoon I made no attempt to go back at all. Home was again a place I was starting to like, getting back was nice and playing with Merlin great fun. He would keep falling over and he loved being tickled and petted. He seemed to grow visibly within a few days and turned frisky and mischievous.

Leaving home I was particularly concerned about the heat. Delhi is sultry in the monsoon, very hot and humid. He sleeps in an air-conditioned room, I thought to myself, and during the day if he is in the fan alone he may get sick. I decide to leave the air conditioner on for him. In the first few weeks I was paranoid about his getting sick, he was so small.

I also started the time tested doggie newspaper routine pushing his nose in his pee if he made a puddle and saying "NO" and then settling him on a newspaper. After a great many misses we'd get it right about two times out of ten and then five times out of ten in a month or so. Success is measured in very small aliquots with very small dogs.

I was still walking in the morning, scruffy tracks and no lipstick !!

Now the walk is done with Merlin in my arms and is more of a slow amble with appreciation of the birds and the trees, rather than a brisk walk with the purpose of exercise. The trees were often washed clean and very green after the rain. I didn't put him down at all and never took him out in the evening. He may pick up an infection I told myself so until we have seen the vet and started immunizing him he doesn't get to walk on mud.

Cleaning the house gave me plenty of exercise for I'd swab the floor in the morning and on coming back from work. Initially using a wiper with a handle I then decided to do it squatting as all the cleaning ladies do so as to work the abdominal muscles too. In the evening Sangeeta would clean up the messes. My house started smelling like more of a hospital than the hospital did, what with the Dettol and phenyl cleanings.

A week or so after I got Merlin, in the evening, the doorbell rings

I wonder who it is for it is yet early for Sangeeta and I open the door to a small boy maybe six or seven wearing a superman tee shirt and short trousers

"Yes?" thinking maybe he has rung my doorbell by mistake

"Good Evening, Auntie. I am Milind and I stay three houses down the lane. You have a Labrador puppy don't you? May I see him?"

Careless parents I think how can they just let him walk into a strangers house like that and then

"Sure, Milind, do you like dogs?"

"Oh yes, we have a Labrador too, You may have seen him when he goes for a walk. His name is Bruno"

If they have a dog why does he want to see mine? He simplifies by explaining

"You know, he is a year old now and he is big, really big. But when we got him he was so small"

Two hands held apart to show me how small.

"*The dog grew too fast for him did it?*" I thought, amused and pleased, with my young visitor

"You can play with him. Just be careful"

He didn't stay long; leaving in 10 minutes saying his parent didn't like him to be out long. He visited us several times after that when Merlin was small, rapidly losing interest, as the dog got bigger.

But it made me realize that I had a new and important identity as far as the kids in the colony were concerned. I was 'Auntie who is Merlin's Mummy' and so popular. For as the dog grew and became playful we invariably had some kid wanting to pet him or to shake hands with him as he started to learn how to do it.

Standing on my verandah in the evening sometimes I had often noticed a young girl on the verandah next door. She was about nine years old and though she looked at the puppy and watched him she never spoke to me. I noticed her mainly for she was quiet and didn't make a nuisance of herself and I rarely saw either parent. Working parents and an only child and lonely I thought to myself. Her evident loneliness touches a chord in me

"Hi sweetheart" I called out to her "What's your name?"

"Natasha"

"Natasha, do you go to school?"

"Yes. Does he bite?"

This conversation is obviously heading towards the dog

"No he is too small as yet, I think"

"Will he let me pet him?"

"Certainly, he loves being petted, he is friendly"

"If I ask my mom and she allows me to, may I have him over in my house for some time?"

Seeing the denial writ large on my face she quickly continues

"You see, I want to show him to my Dad. I want a dog, but he says we can't keep one. If he sees Merlin maybe he will agree to have one"

I truly doubt that one but what am I to say to her

"Ask your Mother and we will see"

Kids are tenacious and my near agreement, as she perceived it, had me a visitor the very next evening. A young woman, very pretty and looking very harassed with Natasha behind her, she said

"Hullo, Good Evening. I am Manisha, Natasha's mother. I hope she hasn't been making a nuisance of herself. She is very keen on having a dog but I have told her we can't keep one but she wants to bring your puppy over"

I can see that she isn't looking forward to the prospect at all but there isn't much I can do about that. The child is polite and pleasant and it would be churlish to refuse. I think it was against the better judgment of both the adults but Natasha took the puppy into her home

"He can make a mess" I call out to her in the hope of deterring her. Did it work? Of course not.

Sangeeta of course has her own take on it

"Better for her to take Merlin there for some time than for her to come and play here. Lot of noise and then we have to look out for her also and they will have to clean the mess he makes."

Smart.

Despite my trying to dissuade her she took the puppy home on several occasions and then finally one day it had to happen. Merlin is next door and a loud scream erupts. I jumped out of my skin and Sangeeta says prosaically

"Kar diya" Done it.

There's a lot of noise next door and the door opens and Natasha rushes out, part laughing and part crying.

"He did his potty on my Daddy's shoes. And he is so mad. He says I have to clean it up"

It had obviously not upset her much but since her Dad was mad it meant no more dog in the house.

I am surprised too. I take the dog out regularly and he has never done his poop in the house, or very truthfully, very rarely. So why now?

I think that was a doggie tantrum.

"Its ok Natasha, he will not be angry for long. Should I send Sangeeta to clean up?"

"No, that's fine, we have a maid too" Oops!!

But she is a smart child and not willing to give up on the dog so easily. I can see her line of thought in her next question

"Do you take him for a walk?"

"Well right now its more like I walk and I carry him but I guess as he gets bigger I will take him for a walk."

"Ok so then, when he starts going for a walk, may I walk with him sometime and hold the leash"

"If my Mommy allows me to?" this as an afterthought

Really, that was smart and forward thinking.

And she did often walk with us in the evening as Merlin grew and I started taking him out on a leash. I would ring her doorbell and she'd come out and walk with us. Walk over and she would go back to her own house.

Contrary to my earlier expectations it was a pleasure having her for company. She is young but sensible and her conversation is often more mature than her years. Coming in one day to wash her hands after we had walked the dog she moves around the house, pausing and looking at the pictures and then

"Who is this?" Looking at a picture of Diven and me

"My husband" I should have said 'late husband' but as usual I have issues with certain declarations and I don't know if she will understand that

"What happened to him?"

"He died" Silence, she is trying to comprehend all this and I tell her

"He was unwell. He had cancer" I tell her a little about his illness in simple words so she can understand. I have never spoken about all this to anyone who I don't know closely and I am surprised at myself.

She listens and then

"I'm sorry, Auntie" and continues, "You must miss him"

This very genuine statement meant more than a thousand silly platitudes but she then questions with a maturity beyond her years

"Didn't you have any kids?"

Out of the mouth of the babes, isn't that a saying

"No"

She trails around looking at all the pictures and asking something about most of them and then leaves and leaving me thinking about something I haven't given any thought to in a long time.

I have wondered sometimes if it would have been easier for me now if we had had a child or children and still the answer eludes me. From a purely selfish viewpoint maybe yes but then this lack had never struck me earlier.

When newly married we had, like other couples, thought we would have kids. It's a natural progression of events isn't it, you get married and then you have children. But nothing happened and when we had been married for three odd years it became somewhat of an issue. We saw doctors and had the requisite investigations and found that nothing was wrong with either of us and there was no reason we couldn't have kids. So we let it be for a while and then for a more while, till it became evident that it wasn't going to happen without more aggressive intervention, if at all.

Possibly we were both complacent to a point, for we were happy and what we didn't have we didn't really miss.

When I suggested that we go to an infertility clinic he said, flippant and downplaying the problem in an attempt to comfort me

"You know, its one of those things, some people have money and some people don't, and some people have kids and some people don't"

"Its not that straightforward" I replied, trifle irately "People ask me so often now and sometimes very pointedly, When are we going to hear the patter of little feet? and stuff like that"

He considers this and then

"And that bothers you? What people are saying? People have to have something to say and something else will interest them and they will forget"

I pushed for the infertility clinic and may have felt the need to do more about it but going to that clinic a few times was actually more degrading than traumatic and I finally decided against it when Diven said to me in all seriousness

"Do you actually want to find a cause, a problem, something wrong? Like say with me or with you so we can have something to throw in each others faces a few years down the line"

No I didn't want to find out. What if they said he could have kids but I cant or the other way round? I definitely didn't want to find that out.

I didn't push it for I was busy and content and if he wasn't bothered I could live with it. In a woman's life the maternal instinct is stronger than that of the male probably and for some time it did depress me, the regularity of my cycles, never late and never missed. But maybe age is a factor in all this and as time went by it ceased to matter to me.

I work with children and often have reason to get really fed up of wailing brats, the tantrums and howls, diapers and rashes and the like. Children to my mind are great and so long as you can have them for a little while and enjoy them, like nieces and nephews, and then they can be sent back to their rightful owners, their parents, and its fine. I didn't have this overwhelming urge to be a mother or to have someone call me 'Mummy'. Maybe some of us just lack this huge maternal instinct or maybe we just didn't pander to it at the right time.

At one point I kind of toyed with the idea of an adoption too but lacked the intense desire for a child which motivates couples who end up adopting. For one, as a couple we didn't want it, only I did and the secondly the thought of taking a child, no idea whose and from where, maybe unwanted and abandoned and God alone knows what lineage did not appeal to me. I admire people who do it and have great respect for them but it was not for us.

I recall speaking to my mother regarding it once. My mother was an obstetrician and treated a lot of patients for infertility. It struck me as ironic that it had to be me, her child, who she could not help. But then I never did want to see her as a patient because she and my husband got along like a house on fire and what would be better at destroying that than a few questions in clinical detail regarding your sex life and similar private moments.

I did not want to do that to either of them so I didn't.

But I did ask her regarding adoption in our context and her answer was simple

"Your husband is unlike most Indian men and you should appreciate that. Another man may have made your life difficult because you haven't conceived. He is happy and does not bother you. Don't create a problem where none exists"

That was true and in retrospect I have often thought that if it had been that important to me I would have pushed it. I didn't really and time just passes so the time for us to have kids also just passed.

And today, talking to Natasha, I realize that that is one thing I don't really regret for I don't believe in regrets. Regrets are a waste of time and self destructive and foolish. What you don't have, you don't miss, I think, so I didn't miss having a child. Possibly it's a great experience but it wasn't written for us and so it didn't happen.

No more mooning around I think and decide to take some pics of the dog. He is beautiful and I want to put his pictures on Facebook. I've been missing on social media for a long time and its time to reappear and this is a good one. So I tell Sangeeta to hold him on her hand so you can appreciate how small he is and then one of him with his teddy. I don't really want a picture of myself on Facebook, I don't look that great.

Nice pictures I tell myself as I upload them
"Merlin, my dog I write, a baby, new addition to my family"
As expected lots of likes and comments follow, most of them pleasant.

My routine now is very different altogether compared with just a few days ago. The dog has truly turned the house topsy-turvy. No floor coverings because he pees all the time and his routine runs my life leaving me tired at the end of the day, too tired to think, too tired to analyze just thankful to be able to lie down in bed and sleep.

I think the first few days with Merlin left me a bit obsessive about feeding, cleaning and forming a routine. We did kind of settle in, often not the way I had planned. Lots of hit and trials and a lot of mess and chewed up stuff, shoes destroyed and clothes with holes in them.

I had cushions peed on and table legs scratched, books mangled and all kinds of varied minor mishaps and major catastrophes too, on occasion, but I have never regretted getting him.

The nicest thing, unarguably, is the way I am greeted when I get back home. The dog goes absolutely ballistic, barking his head off even as I am parking the car and as soon as I open the door he will jump up and then fall down and roll over in ecstasy, his tail wagging madly all the while, his love for me unconditional and undeniable. I may have gone out for only ten minutes but I will always be greeted this way, in a frenzy of excitement and joy.

It's good to be back home these days. Home is home again.

Cheers Merlin . . .

THE WORLD AROUND

"My misery, my blanket
Blinds me so
It's time to shed it"

It's one of those days, when I have a headache, which is steadily getting worse. Migraines come with a warning; a 'prodrome' and I had known a few hours ago that I was heading for one. Knowing this and aware of what can follow I has still ignored the signs and now I curse myself with *"Oh why, why hadn't I taken the medicine then, a few hours ago?"*

Driving home, nauseous and with a head ready to split into two I feel the weight of the world on my shoulders. Busy time at work, all Dengue, Malaria, Swine Flu and what have you, patients sick and parents paranoid, a set of new and relatively inexperienced residents and junior staff and Delhi reeling under various near epidemics that I'm so tired I could just fall down here and sleep for a few hours.

And when I get home I can't even just lie down and sleep. The house will be a mess, dog pee and messy newspapers and

I have to feed the dog and take him out too. If Diven was . . . .
Oh God, why me?

I look at this little talisman hanging on the rear view
mirror of my car. It has a few beads and at the end a big evil
eye, the dark blue and turquoise glass or stone one which is so
popular. Turkish I think. This is indigenously created from a
bead bracelet of mine which broke so he sat and threaded it
into a 'Good luck charm' you know for the car. I finger the
blue glass and my brain relaxes a bit and I think, a cup of tea
and an aspirin before I do the rest of what I have to do.

Clean the mess, then feed the dog, and take him out and
them lie down in the darkened room. Thankfully I nap for half
an hour and the headache dulls. Feeling lazy and lethargic later
in the evening I lounge in the living room, watching Sangeeta
as she cooks.

She is quiet, maybe because she knows my head is hurting
and then paying attention, I realize she is practically attacking
the onion and if she continues to chop it in that fashion she
may well chop off her finger.

Something amiss, I think to myself
"Sangeeta" I call out to her
She turns to me and, I take one look at her face and
comprehend that something is wrong, very wrong
"Sangeeta, Koi problem hai? Is there a problem?"
She bursts into tears. I am shaken, this is so unlike her
"Tell me what it is"
She washes her hands and then stands there wringing
them and starts

"Its Sanjana" more tears

What about Sanjana I wonder. Her daughter is 16 and the one time she came with her mother I got the impression of a shy, pleasant and timid girl.

"Sangeeta make a cup of tea for me and have one yourself too and then tell me"

Finally I get her story

"Sanjana, you know she is in eighth class now and her school is only till eighth. She has to change now for the bigger classes. And the new school, they are asking for so much money, all at once"

A pause and then eyes filling again

"She is intelligent, not like me. She likes to read, she can speak English. I want her to study. She will not cook and clean in people's houses for a living". The tears start afresh

"They are asking for Rs. 20,000. Rs.8,000 for the admission and Rs.12,000 for the first term fee all in advance. We have got only Rs. 8,000 and no more than that. I went to the moneylender but the interest is too high. My husband says we have to think of our son too. We cannot afford so much money for her education"

I find myself not just surprised, but a bit ashamed and horrified too.

What little attention we sometimes pay to people around us. Am I so selfish and so lost in my own small world? Feeling so sorry for myself that the problems around me don't impinge on my cocoon at all? Her tears and near heartbreak, it's for Rs. 12,000?? I am aware that they are not well off, of course, but this is unthinkable. I think back to the amount I spent buying things for Merlin and then feel truly sad about some very basic issues in our society.

The girl child is undoubtedly far less important than the boys in our country in most segments of society and the practice of female feticide is rampant in some states in India. Girls in villages are rarely educated despite the many schemes, the midday school meal program and financial incitements.

Looking at Sangeeta now, I make up my mind and without any frills or catch I tell her

"Don't worry. I will help you. I will give you the money"

The relief in her eyes and the smile that lights up her face is enough to make me feel like a savior of sorts. She says

"Oh thank you so much. Thank you 'Bhabiji'. You will not regret it. I will work very hard and pay it all back. You can cut Rs. 1,000 from my salary every month"

"No Sangeeta you don't understand. I will give you the money. And not just Rs. 12,000, I will give you Rs. 20,000 and I shall be happy to do it. If your daughter wants to study, then make it possible for her. Let her grow up and become something, whatever she want to be"

And I meant it.

I decided at that point that I'd see her daughter through her schooling and then take it on from there if she is still with me, who knows? But upto the tenth is only two years. And in this lot you never can be sure for they may decide to marry off the girl at eighteen. All that I do not wish to interfere with but

I can school her. My little bit for society, I think, but it's not totally unselfish either for it ensures her loyalty too.

Sangeeta was so happy, she positively shone with it.

And I am careful saying it will take day or two to arrange the money. I had been careful to convey very clearly that I don't have much cash on me, always. No jewelry in the house, no displays of money. Why create temptation? People have been murdered for even Rs. 10,000 and I would seem like an easy target for would be robbers and burglars.

This thing about girls, it gets to me. Very pampered in my upbringing and my parents pet it is saddening to realize, this apathy, this attitude towards my sex in our country. Being a doctor you sometimes witness it in the oddest of ways.

I recall a month old male child who was admitted under my care with pneumonia and on discharge they say they will regularly follow up with me for immunization. Not required I say they can do it at a smaller center. In the course of the conversation the father tells me that the baby is one of twins. I'm surprised, the baby is in my care and I have never seen the twin.

"Why haven't you shown the other baby to me?"

"Oh, she's a girl"

In that he has said it all. She is just a girl. She doesn't warrant a doctor or any such frills. The boy will be spoilt rotten and the girl will not even be given the basics. Its as simple as that.

Will this ever change? Not unless we educate our girls and stop treating our boys like little princes around whom the world revolves.

But as for us, Sangeeta is happy and chirpy again and that is a weight off my shoulders. I have given her the money she needed with no strings attached, as simple as that.

And hey, they have found a snake in the colony. It happens sometimes in the rains, possibly water fills the burrows and they are driven out. Largely harmless grass snakes, they nevertheless generate a great deal of excitement. A snake charmer is called to drive it away. That is, in itself a rarity these days like something from a bygone era. Snakes are worshipped in India on a certain days 'Naag Panchami' and the aim is to not kill them by and large.

I hear Sangeeta cheerfully regaling the tale of this snake to Milind who is listening with wide-eyed wonder

"They found a snake in Mrs. Mehra's garden. Called the snake charmer to get it out but they haven't got it yet. Its sooooo long'

Arms wide apart to emphasize,

This snake seems to be growing with every telling. You'd think they had found a dinosaur. But Milind loves every bit of this

"They bite, the snakes 'haan'? Someone could die". Sheer ghoulish delight lights up his face.

Sangeeta in full form, I think to myself, and am pleased to think that I have a small part to play in her happiness

"Yes, sometimes. Be careful when you go for a walk, wear sturdy shoes"

My mind is a bit edgy, restless and I can feel myself thinking, searching in my mind. I cannot say that I am now still in shock or in denial. I am better, sad, yes at times but definitely more settled and yet my mind is not quiet. It's as though I keep pushing something to the back of it and it keeps coming forward. I am not so broken up now, more composed in my grief and able to deal with day-to-day functioning in a fairly reasonable manner.

Looking at Diven's picture I think, yes, there is something I have yet not done and now I have to do it.

I have to go to Srinagar, to Kashmir.

If I have to have peace of mind, a closure of sorts that's where I need to go. I must go. I don't want to. I hate the thought of being in Kashmir without him. Kashmir, our home, and the place which meant so much to him. All during his illness and treatment that's what he had wanted, to go to Srinagar, to go home. And I had thought we would have the time to do it. I was wrong. We were both wrong. The doctors were wrong. He never did have the time. He kept on saying

"When this is over, then, we will go to Srinagar"

"We'll go home for some time"

And I agreed. I'm the doctor and he had full faith in my decisions. Was I wrong in not taking him there when he so wanted to go? But we had no idea that the end would come so soon, so suddenly. We were under the impression that after the treatment, the radiation, he would be better and then the doctors; the oncologists would reassess him, repeat his scans and plan the further course of his treatment.

But that was not to be. A week after completing his radiation he was gone. Gone so suddenly. But yes quickly and painlessly. Maybe that was merciful, I don't know.

Had I known what was going to happen would I have taken him to Srinagar?

That is something I have thought of often. And the answer is no, for that would have meant taking on a kind of responsibility that I cannot imagine. And being completely alone, no family and no friends. And maybe it was good, the fact that we thought till the last day that he was getting better, for we had so much hope. He had improved, his voice had become stronger and his appetite had suddenly reappeared after weeks of picking at his food. But it was not to be.

If I want to really put all this behind me then I have to go to Srinagar. If it's not for me, then it's for him. He loved Kashmir and Srinagar, a place so full of memories, where we both grew up, studied, met, fought, dated, married, where we lived. Every nook and cranny has memories for me and now all of them are hurtful. And they shouldn't be, memories are golden and must be cherished. With the acuteness of grief settling I realize that my memories must be like a stash which has to see me through now and whenever I need them.

My memories have to become my strength, not my weakness and thinking of him I should smile and not cry. For that is life, the joys are mixed with the sorrows, for without that, happiness would have no meaning. Nothing comes without a price tag, not even happiness. If something can give you great happiness then it can break your heart too. And broken hearts must be mended and life lived.

So I decide to go to Kashmir where he'd wanted to retire and grow old. Maybe that was a pipe dream but it had been so dear to us. Losing your dreams hurts for if you can't dream you can't live. And it had been Diven's dream and I will honor it for him.

Dad is not pleased to hear that I want to go to Srinagar. He has always felt that the past should be left there, in the past. I am sometimes inclined to agree but I also know that not going will leave me feeling as though I have left something unfinished.

I think Kiya has been aware that it will come sooner or later, this request of mine. We will go together and she will be my strength.

When the flight takes off from Delhi I am already in tears. Kiya holds my hand, saying nothing. It's a short flight and in an hours time we land in Srinagar. Landing in Srinagar is something, which, is an experience in itself. Kashmir is a valley nestled in the Himalayas and you land flying through beautiful snow clad peaks. We are going in winter so the landscape is going to be bare, bleak.

A sense of peace comes to me when we land there. I have done the right thing in coming here. In a way I have come on behalf of Diven I think, not really myself, for I say to him as I get there

"Diven, you are always in my heart. I love you baby and will say goodbye to Kashmir for you"

And I did just that. The quiet, the silence, the calm, the peace makes for a kindred feeling in my heart and I know I can do it now.

I can go on.

Standing in Gulmarg, which is a hill station in Kashmir valley, and is snow bound for nearly half the year and a famous ski resort I look at some of the places, which have so many memories for me. There is an old graveyard atop a hill in Gulmarg, which has a derelict look for there is no one to look after the graves. And if you look at the names and dates on those graves you realize some are over a hundred years old. Recalling meeting with Diven there years ago, nearly 30 years ago at the age of seventeen I smile to myself. I have forgotten my tears.

Something's hold up with time, don't they sweetie, and here I am 30 years later.

For some reason that trip to Srinagar, though it now looks nothing like it did when we grew up there, put things in a better light for me. That is life, no guarantees. And in any relationship one person will have to go first and leave the other alone. How much time we have together is something no one can predict but if it is a time filled with love and good times then a short time is also acceptable I decided. Will have to count life with the preciousness of my memories rather than the numbers of our years together.

Leaving Kashmir I knew that maybe I will not be back in a hurry and that too is something sad. On the flight I sit already half in Delhi and planning. Taking a paper napkin I start to make a list of things that I need to do. I'm an inveterate list maker and ticking things off gives me great satisfaction.

So I start

1.Vet for Merlin

Kiya leans over my shoulder to read what I am writing and says

"Maybe you should put your own self higher on the list than Merlin"

As I look askance at her she continues

"Have you seen yourself in the mirror lately? You are greying, your hair is a mess and when did you last go to the parlor?"

I put a hand to my hair, possibly its messy for its curly and frizzy and I haven't been too concerned and parlor

"Maybe a month, no two months ago"

And so my list gets another item and that is, what is the term used these days, oh yes

2.Give myself a makeover

So I will attack these issues ASAP but now I am looking forward to seeing Merlin wondering how I am going to be greeted. After all this is the first time he has been without me and for four whole days at that.

I haven't overestimated my welcome. Merlin practically jumps out of Sangeeta's arms as he greets me. Ecstatic with joy, he jumps, rolls over and I am hardly able to hold him, he is so excited and trying to get at my face and lick me. Normally my dog is not licky, thank God, but special meetings, after so long call for a real doggy greeting. And after that for the next few days I had a dog that would not let me out of his sight. If I go to the washroom the dog is sitting outside and follows me from room to room. It is in point of fact a real nuisance for when I turn around half the time I am in real danger of tripping over the silly animal.

Taking my 'to do' list seriously I look myself over in the mirror to see what I can do to improve myself. Maybe I have grown used to myself for I find an older, greyer and more serious visage, which seems to be me. What happened to that cheerful smiley face? Well let's give ourselves a shot at improvement. Turning my back to the mirror I crane my neck to see my posterior. And what happened to the once upon a time called 'J Lo butt'. Gone, I think, possibly seems a bit broad in the beam, I observe and I need to move it.

Color my hair, I think to myself remembering a very old Billy Joel number which goes 'Just the way you are' in which he claims 'don't go trying some new fashion, don't change the color of your hair' and suddenly its fun, what I want to do.

I want to look nice. I want to look attractive.

I decide that I will choose my hair color and then take it to the parlor. Looking at the choices I am tempted, Blonde? Who wouldn't love to be blond for some time, but I doubt if my skin can take it and purple?? Oh wow, wow I'd give a year or two of my life for that but I don't think my work place can tolerate it and then Black I think. But I've had black hair all my life and I want something different now, a change, something to liven up things.

After endless rumination I decide on a shade of Burgundy and I am convinced that I am being very adventurous. Oh ye of little faith, think of me, I'm like in the previous century. Everyone is colored and streaked and permed and what have you and here I am, having kittens at the thought. Leaving the parlor I preen with my new hairdo and hair color and turn my head this way and that seeing how the light catches the red in my hair. Very nice.

I think I will get some new clothes too for now I am wearing more western clothes and I don't have a large wardrobe of those. It's a bit crazy isn't it, that Diven didn't like my saris, and I wore them all the time and now that he isn't here I am wearing what he likes. Strange things happen don't they or maybe I am subconsciously pleasing him, becoming what he wanted me to be.

Rebellion in reverse.

Anyway, the next day, I walk into hospital and rounding on my patients, patiently wait to receive a compliment on my new hair look. Doesn't happen. Nobody notices anything at all. What am I here?, a part of the furniture that nobody seems to notice anything at all.

Having worked in the same place for over ten years gives a degree of familiarity that goes beyond professional and as such a degree of informality too. I call out to our head nurse or the team leader as they are called these days

"Seema"

"Yes, Ma'am"

"Seema I wanted to ask you?" I pause and wonder how to phrase my question

The girls are used to me and so I get the answer before I can ask the question

"Ma'am it's looking nice. Your face is looking fresher and younger. You have put henna in your hair"

I know how a balloon feels when it's deflated.
Maybe I should have gone blonde after all.

Makes one realize though that one agonizes over the most trivial of issues, and that's especially true of women, our hair and our skins and how fat we are looking and whether our behinds are too big or our look too over the top or whatever and most of the time it isn't even noticeable.

Keeping this concept firmly ensconced in my mind I go shopping for clothes and find again that so much is available. India has changed. From a time when it was rare to see married women in anything other than a sari we now have trousers and tops, the Indian 'salwar kurta', dresses and even shorts.

Thinking back to some incident with Diven, as I am wont to do often I recall commenting on seeing a woman in a grocery store dressed totally inappropriately in a particularly low cut and daring sari blouse. She wasn't young, maybe mid forties but we were younger and I said

"Its strange that women have no idea what to wear and where"

And my husband replies

"Do you realize that when they are young, they are newly married and they have a mother-in-law practically breathing down their neck? Dependent even for pocket money. And then they have one kid and then another kid so that by the time they are forty the kids are teenagers and the husband isn't bothered any longer. She is probably living out her youthful fantasies now."

Maybe that is true. By the time we get to our forties we are more financially independent and also more confident. We I think have also learned that it is difficult to please every one. Diven was often older than his years and observed people closely and noted even the tiniest details whereas I am least likely to have been bothered.

Well now I am doing something very similar. Having dressed very conservatively for work in most of my career I am now planning to change to a more comfortable and less strict dress code. Is it age or defiance? Possibly neither, just a desire for some change. Change is inevitable sometimes or stagnation results I defend my choices.

Now I enjoy myself, shopping with a vengeance, having a ball. Haven't been spending much so there is no need to feel guilty. Neatly tailored trousers and clean-cut full-sleeved shirts are a pleasure.

Some open toed sandals and a pair of red shoes. That last one was a mistake but then so what, maybe I will never wear it but what the hell.

What the hell, I convince myself, I like red shoes.

Fashion is sometimes incomprehensible and even borders on ridiculous, I think looking at some of the clothes. From tops cut with uneven borders, to kurtas with tassels like curtains and lots of glitter and beads it's all available. And there is something, which is on par with the 'bell bottoms' of the seventies, equally atrocious and oh so very popular. That is the so-called 'jeggings'. If no one has heard of it, it is something like a glued on trouser, a cross between jeans and leggings giving it the name. All colors and even prints and all kinds of fabric from cotton to satin and from khakis to formal blacks, are available.

Holding one such 'jegging' up, I wonder what appeals, maybe it is meant for the teenagers but everyone including the fat matrons with kissing thighs are wearing this, sometimes with absurdly short tops.

I have recently read in a medical journal that when we see ourselves in a mirror our brain makes us perceive ourselves seven to eight times more attractive than we actually are. Some kind of defense mechanism I think.

Refusing to dwell on this particularly amazing fact with respect to myself I figure I do understand why all the healthy female population in India is wearing this thing. I'll give it a miss.

I end up eating at Mac Donald's and pig out on French fries. And follow it up with a chocolate pastry at the patisserie. I seem to be losing it all over again, I think, doing all the wrong things, no Kiya to provide some common sense.

It's all for a good cause.
Me.

Driving back I take the long route home. There is a short route through a commercial area and a longer one which is often called the hill route for it goes through the outskirts and is winding and undulating and the closest to a hilly terrain in this part of the world. There is a shooting range on it and it was done up in the 2010 commonwealth games for the championships. The road is as smooth as a carpet and a pleasure to drive on, the greenery a delight and a change. As I round a bend I see something, oh my.. There it is. . . . .

A peacock dances on the side in the field, it plumage fully spread out, moving in tune to some silent melody its feathers moving from side to side. The colors are incredible, blues to gold, emerald green to black and all tones and hues intermingled. I slow down and then finally stop to watch it. It is amazingly beautiful and I am entranced by it. It isn't a rare sight but it can amaze you every time and leave you completely spellbound. Standing there on the lonely road nearing home at dusk I am willing to accept that the divine exists.

God has his ways.

Yes I accept that God must be having some reason for doing what he does to us. Maybe there is a larger picture in front of him that we do not see. Or the reason or explanation I have is much simpler and acceptable to me.

You see some people are good, really good. And now I don't mean good looking or the do gooders. I mean people who are truly good at heart and different from the rest. Wishing no one harm and going about their lives in whatever way. And like the rest of us God needs good people there. There, up in heaven.

That's why he calls them back young
Only the good die young.

I try to decide to go to a temple but really I am not ready for it. My faith in God is shaken and I do not know if it will ever be the same again. I am not willing to go if I can't believe and not for ceremony as is so common in India. I don't need to show anyone anything.

I realize I am changing too. Undeniably.

Merlin is softening something in me, maybe warming my heart. Truly no one can love you the way a dog does. Unconditional and unswerving loyalty is something humans could learn from them.

My doggie is bigger and now we are able to go for walks. When I speak to him he nods his head as though he is listening and if I just call his name he will race to me from wherever he is. And tumble and fall in his excitement.

And he has turned chewy. He can chew anything; he is not picky at all. Shoes, socks, books and newspapers are his favorites though expensive clothes and curtains are not far behind.

We still need to find that vet.

My problems certainly have changed, haven't they !!

A DIFFERENT PERSPECTIVE

"When reason fails to comfort
We turn to the little known"

The Pediatric ICU is hectically busy. There is an atmosphere of waiting and apprehension, which overhangs the usual efficient buzz and creates a visible stress among the nursing staff and the patient attendants alike. There is relative silence for the patients are all very sick and for most part on ventilators and the usual crying, wailing and tantrums are completely absent. It is November and the tail end of the so-called Dengue season. We have lost two patients to this scourge in the past two days and many others across the county have faced a similar plight.

Times like these are when being a part of the ICU services can play havoc with the nerves and the constant ongoing fight to beat disease and death sometimes seems a futile exercise. For the demon wins and often. Functioning as one of the big tertiary care referral centers we have the sickest of the sick patients, and children at that. The look is almost like that of a science fiction movie, the ventilators at the side of sedated sleeping children, very much like little angels lost in a monstrous haze of machines.

The monotonous whirring of the ventilators is punctuated by the beep of the monitors and intermittently interrupted by the sound of the alarms. The nurses scurry from bed to monitor or stand at the foot end of the beds, standing vigil by their precious charges and moving only to administer the medication or adjust the covers. The doctors appear busy and over worked and the usual bonhomie and careless chatter is conspicuous by its absence.

I am used to this and in point of fact it may not be completely wrong to say that at times this is our milieu and it is like home to our minds. The struggle to treat our patients, the fight with disease and disability, the seemingly thankless tasks at times, the long years of study and the hard hours, the commitment, the fatigue and the stress, the loss of a social life seems worthwhile when our patients head towards recovery and out of this domain, the ICU.

The stress tells on everyone, the doctors, the nurses and the parents and relatives of the patients. Waiting and relatively helpless, unable to contribute to the care of their babies at this point, the parents watch with ill concealed tension and apprehension as the doctors go about their work, desperate to hear words stating an improvement or stabilization of their child's condition and at the same time dreading to hear the worst.

Resorting to all manner of things for comfort, from prayer to giving of alms, from speaking to religious preachers to resorting to quacks.

At all these times all the alternative systems of medicine thrive from medicines given in little packets to bring down fever to garlands of ginger and garlic on children with jaundice to the juice of the papaya leaves to bring up the platelet count in patients suffering from Dengue.

Any and every possible measure, which may bring some kind of improvement, is tried, trips to religious places are planned and large donations promised to the Gods.

In India, 'Gurus', 'Baba' and various 'God men' are, if not the norm, then certainly not unusual and are among the various sources of much following at these trying times. It's not unusual to see at the bedside of sick children pictures of a God, or a Guru, a religious book, sometimes a cross or a 'Taviz', which is a talisman from a religious guru. This kind of trying situations are singularly unifying as caste, creed and religion are forgotten and people from all walks of life rally together to provide comfort to each other. I have seen lifelong friendships mature and sustain among the mothers of children who have been hospitalized in the PICU at the same time.

As doctors it is our duty to not only treat our patients but also to be able to communicate well with the parents, provide support where we can and in the event of bad news be able to deal with the situation with sympathy and hopefully comfort. Be somewhat human and humane. It is often said that doctors are unsympathetic and blasé for they deal with death all the time and so get used to it.

You can never get used to death. Having been a doctor for many years I can say that death is to us the ultimate enemy, an evil we fight to the last breath. No doctor, ever, wishes to lose a patient but yes we are often aware of the reality of the situation and when it is not possible to give the outcome in stark words the truth may be cottoned a little to make it easier to bear.

We are used to unusual requests from our patients' parents and grandparents and make every effort to honor them from using holy waters, the ashes from holy shrines to various rituals and customs they may want for their children's likely betterment.

Leaving the ICU at the end of a particularly taxing day I am stopped on my way out. A young mother looking very harassed and yet composed asks me

"Doctor, excuse me, may I speak to you for five minutes?"

"Certainly"

"As you may be aware I am Adya's mother, the baby in 4562."

"How can I help you? We are doing the best we can for her and I hope she will be better soon"

Knowing full well that we may be seeing some very hard times here I can offer her no more than that.

"I have a request," she says and I wait for her to continue, "We have full faith in your treatment" she goes on "but I wish to ask for permission to bring in a healer. She comes highly recommended and she heals with reiki and crystals. I has spoken to her and she wishes to do it at Adya's bedside. For that we need your permission to allow her to come into the hospital. Would you sanction that?"

I do not see any reason to deny her wish. Why wouldn't you be looking for any way, which may possibly work when the doctors offer such harsh and grim prognoses?

"Please go ahead. Try to do it during working hours so I can allow it."

Rules are strict for ICU visitors and so I will have to give permission for this.

"Ok doctor, thank you. We will do it tomorrow. We will fix a convenient time after your rounds"

"Done"

As I move along a part of my mind is skeptical for we all know that doctors come in for a great deal of flak at these times. Medical treatment is sometimes prohibitively expensive and when there are poor outcomes there is often a great deal of resentment at the time of billing.

As tired as I am I feel a bit of resentment too, and that surprises me, for I am usually very tolerant of all these idiosyncrasies. I can understand the sentiments that prompt these people to turn to the 'Healers' and 'Gurus' and 'God men' and such like it's just that it will often lead to a portrayal of us, meaning the medical profession in general, in a poor way.

For if the child gets better the sentiment is going to be

"See going to 'guruji' worked. He saved our child as he had said he would" And if by chance, the patient does not make it and succumbs to the disease it is likely to be

"We took our child to the best hospital in Delhi but the doctors there could not save her"

Part of life, I philosophize to myself, and head home, looking forward to an evening with my dog and hopefully some good food.

During busy work times it is impossible to 'switch off' after you leave hospital and in the course of the evening, which is punctuated by frequent calls from hospital, all these things stay with me even as I relax, listen to some music and play with my dog.

Merlin is now good company and a fun dog sometimes as I have been giving him some basic training and he follows commands to some, his own mood dependent, basic issues. Teaching him to 'Sit' took a long time since he was so excited looking at the dog biscuits, which come as a reward for getting it right that he rolls over with joy. So I have to pick him up, and pat him on his rump and then start again 'Sit Merlin' and then sometimes he does, but I am not sure whether it happens by chance or because he understands the command. But it makes the evening enjoyable.

Sangeeta's take on it is somewhat different. She is convinced that the dog 'understands English' for he will not listen when she tells him in Hindi. The amount of time I spend teaching him a command in English is of no consequence apparently.

In the night too my mind is not really quiet. My dreams buzz with the beeps and alarms and half my mind is on my phone. Intensive care is very hard work and I am now often more tired than I can remember being earlier. The fatigue is actually more mental and emotional, for dealing with death and issues relating to it on a day to day basis leads to a sort of worry and handling negative emotions all the time leaves it mark on you. I think you start to get compassion inertia, can't always have your heart hurting for the world at large, all the time. I don't know.

I recall what Diven used to say to me and now I wonder what's happening to me. At the end of tough days he is always on my mind. After a particularly trying day I'd often be full of energy and maybe slightly edgy and Diven said once

"Your work seems to give you a pure adrenaline high and you thrive on it, don't you?" And that was so true. But now I often feel that a distinct low, a drain of energy and a kind of lethargy and listlessness follow the adrenaline surge.

Could just be fatigue I wonder, or is it more serious, like possibly heading towards a 'Burnout'? We do know about these issues but often feel they won't happen to us.

"Is that what it's all about?"

Or is it simply the big 5-O looming? Not a joke I think, half century?

Whatever the reason I find I suddenly want something more, something else and decide I will give it some thought at leisure when this work scenario lightens up.

Sara has completed her work tenure with us and is planning to head back home which is a town in Punjab. Punjab is one of the northern states in India, largely agricultural and very affluent. She has been offered an attachment in a new and upcoming hospital and is considering it seriously. I decide to have her over for a meal since she has been keen to see Merlin and it will give me a way to sound her plans too.

Over the evening, after much a fuss has been created over the dog, who simply loves being petted and is sitting happily in Sara's lap I broach the more sensitive issues

"What's happening in your life Sara?"

"My parents are very keen that I go back," she says "My divorce has become official and they wish that I should now go and stay with them" She doesn't sound too keen so I ask her

"What is wrong with that? I think you have a good offer in the new hospital, don't you? And it is in your hometown so it would make sense to stay with your parents" This is not an unusual situation in India so I cannot understand what is worrying her. She replies

"Yes, Ma'am the work will be good and I am looking forward to it actually. A more independent functioning and a busy hospital"

"So what is bothering you?"

"Now that I am single again my parents will start matchmaking for me and I don't want that"

Seems like a good idea from where I am looking, for I can understand what must be on their minds. In our country, marriages are often arranged and they work out well enough. Of course, now, love marriages are becoming more common and are also accepted where maybe fifty years back they were the exceptions.

And since she has been through a bad experience why blame her parents for wanting something tried and tested for the next time. I try and talk some sense into her

"Sara, I don't thing you should be so averse to it. They will try to find someone compatible, won't they? They aren't likely to pressurize you into marriage with just anyone. You should be open to suggestion I think"

Her face reflects her indecision and she says

"I will never love anyone else"

That statement sounds so young and so defiant that I back off a little for I don't wish to push her the way she feels her parents are doing.

The Indian parents I think, at heart, are still conservative and wish to see their daughters married and happily settled, no matter their educational or career status. And old habits and ideas die hard and if a young woman is unattached there will be matchmaking. Doesn't seem anything to fuss about to my mind.

And so I tell her as best I can

"Sara, I can understand what you are saying, but there is no harm at all in meeting some young man your parents choose for you. Meeting is not a commitment. You should be open to it, for you never know, may just turn out to be someone nice. Love happens slowly and sometimes it doesn't happen at all. So many arranged marriages in our country and they work well enough"

"And what about you Ma'am?"

I am taken aback. We were talking about her, weren't we?

"What about me?"

"I mean you should also think about someone, go out a little more and maybe a.. A" she pauses and thinks and chooses her words carefully "'Friend'?? You know to go out with or maybe dinner or a movie or something"

"Sara, this is silly"

"No Ma'am it is not silly. I know I may not meet you again at least for a while and I love you so I am saying it. Think about it Ma'am"

She seems to have effectively reversed tables on me, the conversation turns to other topics and she bids me a rather tearful goodbye.

"Hey cheer up, we will meet at conferences and you will come to Delhi off and on. Keep in touch"

"It's been great working with you and I will miss you"

Seeing her off I second her sentiments. We have worked well together and I will miss her too. Sara is a committed and caring doctor and just what the world needs I think. Oh the drinks, in which I indulge rarely, are making me maudlin.

But her statement has planted a small seed in my mind and later falling off to sleep I think about it again and mull it over in my head. This restlessness I feel sometimes, this disquietude, is that the answer? A man?

It is now more than one year since I have been alone and I thought I was managing rather well but now I wonder at my restlessness. I need a bit of a social life maybe but a man?

I miss Diven a lot but will having someone in my life make a difference? And do I really need a man? Like as in sex, for example. Do I miss having sex ? This is something which I have questioned lately. We had a sex life as normal I guess as most people who have been married twenty odd years, which is possibly not a very exciting one. I don't think I miss that much. What I really miss is the cuddling up, the snuggling up to him on cold winter nights or just hugging him at times and holding his hand to talk about the lousy days at work and his making fun of me and making light of so many things. It's him I miss, not a man and so I doubt if a man will help.

And in any case where am I to find this man for I go out little and he is unlikely to drop from the sky. Hospital? Oh boy if I start viewing my colleagues as potential boyfriends I could really land trouble for work is largely a male oriented domain and it is easier if they think of me as 'One of the boys'. I don't want it any different there. This is no answer to my present dilemma whatever name I give to it.

I am kind of looking forward to seeing this 'Reiki' giver or 'Faith healer' who is coming to see Adya tomorrow. And I am not disappointed.

This lady comes, a rather stylish and fancily dressed vision, in a pale pastel glittery sari, long dangling crystal earrings and many bracelets jingling on her wrists.

Would they have any faith in a doctor who looked like that, I wonder?

The atmosphere is solemn and she sits by the child's bedside and seems to be in deep contemplation, murmuring or chanting under her breath while waving what looks like a wand in crystal over the child's head. After a few minutes of this she lays a complicated pattern of crystals near the head end and asks for permission to leave it in place for a few hours. We allow her to do it. She follows this up by a request for incense, which is more difficult for us, and we have to deny her. Too much oxygen floating around in the air, it could possibly be dangerous we tell her. She is efficient in her working and after some more incantations she leaves in a cloud of expensive perfume.

We watch her leave, not sure of her credentials but aware that she has made a considerable impression on most of the onlookers.

At any given time the ICU patients are a mixed bag with some new and acutely ill babies and the odd one, which has been there for a while. And as this lady leaves, the mother of one of the more chronic patients, comes and asks me

"Doctor, who is she?"

I am really tempted; 'fraud' and 'quack' are the first words that come to my mind. But no, that's unfair I think. Just because she is attractive and does not look like a harassed doctor and smell of antiseptic is no reason to hold her profession against her

"She is a faith healer" is my reply

"May I consult her for Siddhanth?" that's her son and he has been here for nearly six weeks without too much improvement

"I am sure you can" I answer her.

These little events are like waves in a pond, starts like a small ripple and then spreads all over the place. Before we knew it this lady was coming in for three or four of the patients daily. When I ask the parents about her fees I am told

"Rs. 3,000 per visit"

Really, that takes the cake, I think to myself. So for seeing her four patients she gets Rs. 12,000 and what do we have to show for it?

Anyone may think I have no faith in all this. That would not be the complete truth but in the ICU it does sometimes upset me for it detracts from our importance. The responsibility, the blame is all ours, and the credit may have to be shared is what are my subconscious fears. Medicine, the way it is these days, has the lawyers not so far behind while the so-called 'faith healers' answer to no one.

Not a fair game truly.

I think we all do believe and understand that science does not have all the answers and that there are situations where the turning point is often precipitated by events we neither understand, nor can predict or circumvent. Hopeless patients will turn around and make a recovery and someone on the mend may slide downhill so calamitously that no one can do a thing to help, certainly not the medical profession. It is not for us to believe in miracles nor for us to promote such ideology for our profession is a science, but, as a witness to some very unlikely survivals we are willing to make place in our minds, for the little known, or to accept that we do not have all the answers.

My mind wings to another time, another place. A young girl waiting on a pleasant, sunny afternoon in Gulmarg to meet up with her beau. Secret meetings, romance, golden moments and happy memories. I was eighteen and waiting to meet Diven in the graveyard on top of the hill in Gulmarg. A beautiful day, azure blue sky forming the perfect backdrop to the tall and stately pine trees, flowers blooming making the air fragrant and the atmosphere romantic.

The graveyard has stone headstones with inscriptions of a day and age, bygone. From the time of the British Raj and forgotten since, the grass long and uncut, carpets of daisies blooming, untrodden, untouched and pristine. I can see down the hill as I wait and sitting on the grass, close to a grave I weave a daisy garland and put it on my hair, enjoying myself. I still have a photograph like that, long hair in two braids with daisies on my head taken with a black and white camera roll. I see him coming up the hill, tall and lanky, overlong hair and slightly slouchy as he always was, a camera slung over one shoulder and carrying something in his hands, a book possibly for me.

As he reaches me he smiles, a bit shy, Diven's smiles were always a bit shy while mine never were and hands me a rose

"Hi baby, its good to see you"

"Hi"

As we sit and talk here he asks me, with a nod to the package in his hands

"Guess what this is?"

"No idea, is it for me?" I ask

"No, its something Rene got for me, from the United States. I brought it to show you"

"So, what is it?" Our relationship still very new and I haven't yet become aware of his taste for the unusual or often bizarre as I later thought often, as his wife.

But then way back he was my boyfriend, sweetheart and so, so sweet.

"It's a Tarot Deck"

I hadn't ever heard of a tarot deck till then and this was 'The Grand Etiella' a very old pack and as he tried to explain to me I looked at the cards, the fascinating pictures, the numbering very similar to a deck of playing cards, the imagery intricate and colorful.

That was my introduction to the Tarot and though interested in a vague way, my interest was not really caught till much later, nearly fifteen years later when I first bought myself a deck and that was the 'Enchanted Tarot'. I now have many decks, the 'Raider White' which is an all time classic and the 'Mystic Tarot' and two other ones.

Strangely, for I haven't met too many men who'd want to have anything to do with a tarot deck, Diven was always a believer though he made no attempt to do a reading. His way was to pick a card at the start of the day to figure how the day would go.

I recall wandering around the graves reading the headstones as he explained the concept of the cards to me. Gulmarg and that graveyard have always been special. It's still there, old, sleeping in the sun or buried under the snow and a place for rendezvous' and romance.

Way later I studied them in detail and, though I still hesitate to say this in public, would swear by the cards. The cards are always right but the we don't most of the time read or interpret them correctly. I have used them to meditate and to try and read the future, which I often feel they get right.

I did, like all tarot enthusiasts, go through a short phase where I did readings for a few close friends but it took a lot of effort and time and I didn't have any to spare. Reading for other people, I came to understand, is partly about the cards and partly reading faces or expressions which give you a very clear idea whether you are headed in the right direction or not.

Anyway for myself I do believe to a great extent. When faced with a problem you can lay out the cards and they will tell you the lie of the land. A lot of interests are phasic, I mean you may go through a time when you read them often and for ages they are not of interest to you.

At one point of time, a bad phase, I repeatedly picked the 'Ten of Swords', one of the worst cards in the pack and synonymous with 'Ruin'. And my husband told me

"Stop psyching yourself. And stop seeing the cards. You are hell bent on expecting the worst and then it is likely something bad will happen"

Nothing really happened then because the cards are not absolute in their meaning, assuming one can interpret them correctly. In a manner of telling they give you an idea regarding a situation and not the outcome in absolute terms. Often they may indicate that your stance in a matter is wrong and that means changing your attitude can change the outcome.

They leave room for a lot of interpretations and observations.

An easier way is to use one card to meditate or to foretell the day, leaving the complicated spreads to the experts. If it's a bad card one should be careful over the day, for maybe you are prone to trouble. If it's a good card then you will have a good day. Or so they say.

Maybe all of us are superstitious to some extent and I haven't seen the cards for a while. Time to unearth them for a look –see.

Mundane matters too need attention.

We, Merlin and I have been to see a vet. I don't think he likes me very much, the animal doctor I mean, for I am critical of him and question a great deal. He tells me my dog needs vitamins and Calcium and supplements, which does not go down very well, I mean I am feeding him so well. I think he needs only his immunization and that too is arguable for there is a huge lobby against the vaccines for children today, does the same apply to dogs? The dog senses something funny and absolutely refuses to enter the clinic, dragging and pulling at his leash so I finally I have to pick him up.

He weighs about 6 kg now and I have no idea what he weighed when I got him. He was smaller I said.

Overt professional rivalry over a dog.

How different can a dog be from a child I figure but obviously the vet differs. Needs shots every month for 3 months and some deworming later.

So far, so good.

I hope Merlin stays well so we don't have to see the vet more often than we have to. We, meaning Sangeeta and I have another concern, which we haven't mentioned to the doctor. We have been to see him two times over two months and both times were for injections and so maybe the dog and both of us somewhat scared. The issue is that, the dog pees squatting and never raises his leg or whatever way dogs are supposed to. Not that I want him to really because he still pees on newspapers inside the house and I don't want him dirtying the chair legs but still I am wondering how he is going to get to doing it the doggie way.

It was a milestone of sorts, the first time Merlin peed on a tree. I am so used to his sitting down to pee that when he circles a tree I just watch and wonder why. He then raised one leg and lost his balance and sat down. Shakily he then raised the other leg, wobbled and finally peed on his own foot !! My poor baby dog, he is so clumsy and I do so love it.

Sangeeta will be thrilled.

This newspaper thing is beginning to get to me. I take him out for a walk and he does his business outside but the whole day he messes up inside and now that he is bigger it's a lot of fluid and takes a lot of cleaning. It's tiring, but how do we stop him from doing it?

Finally it was Sangeeta who figured a solution for our problem. Everyday when I leave for work I leave newspaper sheets in two parts of the room both close to the door and when I come back both are soaked.

Sangeeta has an idea or a brainwave as it turned out to be. She questions me

"What happens if you don't leave a newspaper at all? Where will he do it?" My reply is simple

"I don't want to find out, he could do it anywhere and that will be even more dirty".

But what's the harm in trying for I am an expert floor scrubber in any case now.

Finally, one day, I left the house without putting out any newspaper and at work when I have a break I wonder what I will find when I get home.

The sofa?

The dining table?

My new curtains?

Oh heavens, why did I let Sangeeta talk me into this one?

When I get home I open the door and as is usual, I sniff the air. See what living with Merlin is teaching me. As I smell . . . no stink and so I gingerly step in and look around . . .Nothing.

Nothing

I say to Merlin

"Who did this?"

This is a magic phrase where my dog is concerned, if he hangs his head and looks sheepish you can be sure there is urine somewhere, possibly hidden, as in under the table.

But no, Merlin wags his tail and no sign of any shamefacedness, his whole body moving as he greets me with his usual exuberance.

I can hardly believe it.

My dog is toilet trained.

Such a good boy !!

Sanjana has joined her new school and comes over one day in the evening with sweets for me. When she arrives she bends over to touch my feet as a mark of respect. I try to stop her,

"This is not required"

"Let her do it 'Bhabhiji,' says her mother, you have done so much for her and she may get some good qualities, from you"

Makes one feel humbled.

Milind is now a rare visitor. I think the novelty of the puppy has worn off.

Natasha walks the dog with me in the evenings and loves to have him try out all his tricks 'Sit', 'Wait', 'Stop', 'No', 'Heel' and 'Slowly', she makes him show off in front of her friends and he does follow them, well most of the time he does. She has told me that they may be moving from here after her birthday, which is next month, and she will miss Merlin.

I will miss her too, for I enjoy walking and talking with her.

Merlin loves to 'Shake Hands' and when asked will give first his right paw, then left and then right again. As he grew bigger and heftier that paw can topple a lot of kids with his happiness.

Winter is starting to set in and is a pleasant time. Diwali is late this year and my major concern is regarding Merlin. So much noise with the firecrackers, he will be scared. So I will not go out on Diwali evening. I have got new curtains and cushions for this year and the house will be lit with small mud lamps, which are traditional. Have to please the Goddess Lakshmi.

On Diwali evening I am like a fussy mother hen, watching the dog that is sleeping peacefully as the crackers explode outside.

Will he shake and tremble as Kiya has predicted he will or will he just hide under the bed and tremble with fright? But no, as I watch him closely, almost neurotically I'd say, Merlin shows no sign of fear or the jitters and when I take him for a walk makes a jump for the dazzlers, trying to eat them. He isn't bothered at all. Maybe he is just too dumb to understand the danger for he tries to eat the lights too.

That's my Merlin, he doesn't get scared and he loves everybody. As he got bigger people on the road show a healthy fear of him but he rarely growls and barks only at the cat next door and she doesn't even scramble off.

What with the busy work schedule and winter, my desire to read the cards goes to the back of my mind and life runs it routine way.

It makes me think there's a plan there too. There are times when you are not meant to find out about the future, just to let it unfold and go with it.

Possibly flowing with the tide too has its advantages. No planning, no anticipating.

Just let it happen. *"Que sera sera"*
Whatever will be, will be.

I Can Dance

"If you can walk, you can dance
If you can dream, you can fly"

There is an animal called a Gerbil. It is like a small chipmunk and a popular pet is some parts of the world especially for kids. Gerbils have teeth that never stop growing and they love to shred cardboard and it keeps them happy. Often a gerbil lives its life shredding paper and totally unaware of what's happening around it.

Our lives are sometimes similar. We go about a fixed routine, as good as busily working on a treadmill which is our life and unable to really get off it. But if we take time for a pause and look around there is a world there to discover. It needs courage to venture into the different, unknown and untried.

I cannot say I ever thought of myself as adventurous, not the type to trek in the mountains or sleep in tents and my idea of a holiday is luxury not adventure. Don't ever want to Bungee jump, hate the thought of river rafting, look upon paragliding as stupidity and folks who rock climb as lunatics. So now when this notice catches my attention I wonder why this year I wish to be a part of all this. For this notice I have been seeing every year for more than seven years and it has never meant anything other than to be circulated among the staff in the department.

'NOTICE'

The hospital will be holding its Annual day function of the 25th of May. There will be a cultural program followed by cocktails and dinner. We invite all the staff to participate in the program.

Auditions for the dancing and singing will be taking place on the 15th of April between 3 and 5 pm in the main auditorium. You are requested to encourage workers in the department, senior and junior to participate, and adjust the work schedules accordingly.

Thanking you . . . .

I decide to ask one of my junior doctors about this.

"Would you think of going for this, Vivek?"

Dr.Vivek, one of our pragmatic junior doctors whose major interests in life apart from medicine are cricket and Rajnikant movies could not have been more surprised. He is deliberating on how to refuse without offending me when I issued him an ultimatum

"We will go there at 3 pm, no harm in having a look"

Most of these occasions are meant to be fun and are largely targeted at the junior hospital staff but I want to go, just to be an onlooker as youngsters enjoy themselves and have a good time. The good cheer is sometimes infectious.

As it turns out there is a choreographer who has been taken on for this event, rather over the top for a hospital, but there is a lot of awareness about employees and stress busting techniques these days and I think that is what prompted this experiment.

In the auditorium on that first day the atmosphere is stiff and restrained. The choreographer is a young lady whose name is Noor, which means 'light', light as in illumination and not as in light on one's feet though that would be suited to her as well for she dances with an abandon which is enviable. In this medical and conservative atmosphere she should have stuck out like a sore thumb but I think she comes in more like a breath of fresh air, different and sweet. The boys are staring and the women are, if they would have the guts to admit it, a bit envious. Noor is pretty, she has waist length hair streaked in three colors and is wearing something like a holey tee shirt over very tight tights. No one knows quite what to make of it, us least of all. We have never seen anything like this inside of a hospital premises.

As the proceedings start the idea is for all the participating persons to go up on stage and dance or sing whichever they wish to do. She is encouraging, smiling and telling everyone that they are good but the players are stiff and self conscious. I enjoy watching, for maybe some people are making fools of themselves but there is no harm done.

Noor does not know anyone so when she finally beckons me asking

"Will you be dancing or singing?" I am taken aback.

Before I can reply Vivek says

"Come on Ma'am, be a sport and give it a shot"

I have never danced on a stage since primary school I think and can't sing to save my life. I think this is Dr. Vivek's idea of petty revenge for bringing him here.

I opened my mouth to refuse and then it's like the devil took over, some unknown and hidden entity inside me

"Why not" I think. *"What is the worst that can happen, they will laugh at me, and make fun? Its not as though I am killing off a patient"*

Sometimes I pity us, I mean doctors, our lives begin to revolve around our work and patients so much that there is room for little else.

I went up on the stage and regretted it. I was hopelessly stiff and up there it was enough to paralyze for there were so many people there. But Noor, I think is used to all this. For she boost my morale and makes it easier for all of us by saying

"We will play some music and take you all on stage together and not singly. That way, you can dance and then we will be able to judge and choose"

Well, that was much easier and all one had to do was to sway to music. And they ended up the session with tea and refreshments at 5 'o' clock. I hadn't had such a good time in a long while, or laughed so much in ages, at myself and at the rest of the 'two left feet' crowd.

The next day we, Vivek and I, we both went back there, much to the amusement of our colleagues in the department and I think we got there was a lot of light hearted, good natured fun. I couldn't dance for any practical purpose but my presence had managed to get more of the doctor crowd, some out of sheer curiosity, so Noor pampered me I think.

When finally I did decide to try my hand, or feet as it were, at dancing it was part of a well-choreographed routine to a patriotic song and had the Indian flag as a part of the trappings. Very energetic and easy to do. It wasn't that difficult following her and I tried really hard.

And it was amazing how we all changed. From a set of people who were unwilling to go on the stage on the first day to a set of persons who refused to stop dancing even when the rehearsal was over and the music shut off. That was us by the end of that first week.

All this had been planned to a tee. Imagine this, in a big and busy hospital; there were rehearsals for one month, professional costumes and for the big day there was going to be a team of make up artists as well. It was like being in another world for those two hours every afternoon. A real mixed bag of people, doctors, technicians, the IT lot whom we never meet and two hours of music and dancing, food and laughter, and later as the final approached, costumes, jewelry, hair pieces and make up. We had a ball once we got our bearings. It hardly mattered that we were clumsy, there were just too many of us to be bothered.

Noor, once we got to know her, was very good at her job. She coached us, encouraged us and makes us dance. Initially she asked me

"Ma'am should we have you in the front row?"

This, I think, was deference to my senior position. But I wasn't here to play positions and I said so to her

"No I am too tall for the front. Put me where it's ok with you. I am happy just to be a part of all this"

And I realized that it was not just lip service, I was really happy to be there. Interacting with so many of the girls who I had never known before I made some unlikely friendships which hold even now. They teased me, championed me and made me feel like someone special. There was this incident over the costumes, funny.

Bela, one of the girls in the dance came to me in a tizzy

"Ma'am, please do something"

"About what?" I question her

"About our costumes. They are having a meeting for the selection of the costumes and if you don't intervene we will get the cheapest and the tackiest ones"

I can hardly figure out the relevance of this, but it is obvious that I have to do something about it. So I went for this meeting for the choosing of the costumes and the rest of the paraphernalia. Another surprise, there is an official costume designer making decisions and since our dance has the national flag it is decided that the clothes be simple. Keeping in mind the wishes of my dance friends I decide to give them a fight

"No I think we want more colorful costumes"

Seniority pays you see. Even though they may have thought me eccentric they gave in good-naturedly and we got fancy long skirts with sequins and glitter with matching tops and the veils. Looking at this brightly hued silky, slinky outfit

I can hardly imagine myself so coiffured but the rest of my friends silence my protests. Truly there must be another person hidden inside us sometimes and it makes an appearance when it can find a weakening, something like Herpes Zoster flaring up when the immunity is lowered.

I was fine with the rehearsals but as the day actually approached I had second thoughts.

And third and fourth ones too.

A senior consultant and prancing on stage?

How will that go down with the faculty but when I voice my concerns they are silenced by a lot of young protests

"You are a sport Ma'am and it will be taken in that spirit by everyone"

I am so glad I didn't let my pessimism take over for the day of the program, we had a great time. Done up by beauticians, and that is something I didn't even manage when I got married, and dressed up like a performing troupe, which is what we were for that one day, we gave it our all and got ourselves a resounding applause on an evening filled with goodwill and cheer.

Standing on stage with the bright lights flashing I can hardly believe what I am doing.

What would Diven have said? Laughed, most probably, and that image of him, making fun of me gently, adds something to this moment.

He would have wanted me to do things like this I am convinced, good, wholesome fun and maybe a bit silly. He'd often say

"If you enjoy doing something and aren't hurting anyone in the process, you should do it, and never mind what any one thinks"

I think I am finally getting there, doing more and worrying less.

And smiling, when I think of my sweetheart. Not so that the smiles are not tinged with the hint of tears sometimes which they are, like a rainbow during a drizzle, extra special.

For all of us involved in the program routine workdays were a bit of a let down after the excitement of the last four weeks and I saw the girls occasionally in the tea room and corridors and their quick smiles and greeting make me feel good. Different somehow from my normal self, good, better.

So now I think of adding to my humdrum life something to make it more interesting. Like buying a bicycle for example and that would work if I could persuade or train my dog to run alongside. Does seem overambitious keeping in mind that Merlin is now bigger and also more difficult to manage. Behavioral issues like a difficult child. He seem to be growing at an alarming rate. He weighs nearly twenty kg and this is at less than a year old. Thankfully he is now fully toilet trained but walking him can be a struggle for power. He is strong and when he pulls at the leash I get pulled along and sometimes when we go for a walk it's more like he takes me rather than the reverse. Merlin is so excitable that a cat, a squirrel or even a bird can make him race, making me hold on to his leash for dear life.

He does understand "No" but when excited he seems to turn deaf to my voice.

On a particularly difficult evening when I am being dragged on the leash and shouting at the dog, Milind's mother, comments from her verandah

"Hi, I think Merlin needs a trainer." They have a lab too and he is slow and placid on his walks whenever I have seen him.

"Will that teach him to behave himself or do I have to wait for him to grow some more?"

"He is growing so fast but maybe his brain is not keeping pace" I question and comment half to myself.

She smiles her understanding and replies

"He will at least learn to walk properly on a leash, on your left and not pull at it."

Ok so now we are looking for a trainer. I approach the vet and he hands me a visiting card. Raj, I read, what a fancy name, Dog and Animal trainer.

I called Mr. Raj and fixed up with him. He will come 3 times a week, for half hour stretches and he will charge Rs. 6000/-, looks like this is good business.

When he does show up he is dressed up like a modern mafia person with greasy slicked down long unkempt hair, low-slung jeans and a lot of chains and danglers. Merlin is for once quiet and not his usual frisky self and goes off on his leash for his training session.

Every time Mr. Raj brought the dog back, he was breathless and panting. The dog I mean and he said he makes him run for exercise. I considered following them on the sly but that would be difficult and impractical. Something didn't quite gel with me and I requested him to do him class in the front yard in my presence. For some reason, Merlin was scared of him, I realized, his behavior subdued in his presence and his usual mischievousness tamed but later he often was back to normal often ill mannered self.

I had no answers and I felt that he hit the dog to train him. When I confront with this he says that to teach animals we sometimes need to instill some fear in them. No I didn't like that at all and finally I tell him after a month that I cannot afford him and that I will try to teach the dog myself.

I didn't have any good reason other than the fact that Merlin did not like him.

And I trust my dog's judgment.

It is true; I do trust Merlin's judgment. It's infallible. If Merlin doesn't like someone you can bet your last buck he is justified. As was the case with the man who came to repair the microwave and to let him into the kitchen I had to put Merlin on a leash. He barked wildly and growled, a low pitched and ominous sound, which worried me. Because Merlin created such a racket I played safe and called the store, which had supposedly sent this man. I receive a simple reply

"We haven't sent anyone"

"But, but'

I turn around and that fellow is gone. I don't know how he knew where to come and say just the right things but scams like this abound in this area. Possibly they have some dubious associates.

Now I am convinced about my dog's instincts, if he doesn't like someone I will not let them into my house or my life.

The last month of dancing had left me with the feeling of wanting to do more in life for after all that excitement life was ordinary and a bit of an anticlimax. I have made it a point to go out at least once a week often with Kiya or then with my sister and I am planning to watch movies in the theater, alone. Well this is only planning so far.

Possibly the dancing episode wrought in me a larger change which I didn't really realize at that time for change creeps up slowly and sometimes uninvited. For a start if I'd had to do this two years earlier I would never have done it. Cannot come up with a concrete reason but most likely a great deal to do with what others are likely to think. What others? We may not realize it but the world around us governs our life as completely as if it were written in rules. You conform; behave as expected, dress as expected and live as you are required to do. Change isn't easy; wanting something and getting to do it are two different things altogether.

We create our own limitations.

Nobody really tells us what we cannot do as adults but we live our lives doing so much in the 'expected' way. Well I am now, I think, rebelling against this and how it will work out no longer bothers me. Maybe I am older and wiser, or just dumb.

As I walk out of an OPD consultation Dr. Shekhar, one of our surgeons, confronts me. Surgeons are deemed 'Gods' by medicine and that's because the physicians often just think and discuss while the surgeons 'Do'. In our profession many lines are natural protagonists and that would be surgeons and physicians, the clinicians and the pathologists, the obstetricians and the pediatricians for a start. Working together and yet often at loggerheads. Needing to give space and hating each other at times. As I see him stroll towards me with every intention of speaking to me I can hear my mind say

"*I really don't need this one now*"

My mind is of course no deterrent at all for Shekhar reaches me and

"Hi, how is life and how is work?"

Approaching me he casually slings his arm around my shoulders. It isn't that huge a gesture but I dislike his familiarity. Without being rude it is difficult to dodge this one. I keep my cool

"Oh the usual, same, same"

He leans closer, smiling and says

"I think we should end our differences you know. Maybe we can discuss it over drinks one of these days in the evening"

Sometimes you do a lot of thinking in just a second. I wonder what this is, an olive branch or a pass? I could be making a mountain out of a molehill and then I'd feel like a fool. No, this is not a come on, it is more like psychological warfare. Thinking how much pleasure it would give me to just slap his face or snub him I play safe and smiling very sweetly I reply

"Sure, one of these days" and, sliding out from under that arm I back off.

I have no idea what I have conveyed to him, but likely he gets the message. I know what that one meant, it was just testing waters and not a pass, not in the truest sense of the word though it may have worked that way too. No, it was much smarter than that; it was an open invitation and nothing that on repetition could be deemed offensive.

But it puts me thinking.

Would he have dared to talk to me this way two years ago, I think, or is it just some signal I am giving out, that I am more vulnerable now, more likely to be pressurized, more available?? Our insecurities can leave us open to demons that find a hold to torment. This small incident did worry me for impressions are important. I want to think this is a one off gesture but am forced to be more realistic.

I had thought my age gave me a natural immunity but somewhere the signals are mixed. Maybe my good cheer lately is something that I should dampen a bit.

It is always the small things that bother us.

I think when we train we are made to live in an illusory world. Idealistic young doctors begin practice in the real world, poorly equipped to deal with real medicine and harsh reality. Knowledge and caring are not enough, there's much more needed, interpersonal skills, person handling and street smartness, which we are never taught. We learn as we go along and some become good doctors and some are just caught in the large-scale consumerism of selling medicine. It would be unfair to say that being women makes a difference in medicine but it would be a lie to say that glass ceilings do not exist.

I have begun to feel a bit disillusioned with my line of work. Is it a part of my overall mind searching or something more, who knows?

I decide at this point to give a little more back to the profession that has given me so much and in doing so find a way to divert my mind from the professional dissatisfaction that hits me so often these days.

I decide to go to 'Parivartan'.

'Parivartan' is an NGO which takes care of orphaned or abandoned girls aged six to eighteen years and it was started a year or two ago by someone who I know rather well. He has lost a child to muscular dystrophy and got motivated to help children. With my schedule this project never did catch my attention and even now I am a bit divided for this place is likely to be a huge emotional drain.

The last time I went to one of these so-called welfare projects was a sore disappointment with a poor level of care for the children and a lot of talk. NGO's often manage to garner a fair amount of money and are popular for all the wrong reasons.

I am pleasantly surprised to find Mr. and Mrs. Naidu; the organizers spend a great deal of time there and have made it a point to be there on the day of my first visit. They seem to be genuinely committed to their wards. I am going in the capacity of a medical advisor and shall go twice a month to see the girls who are unwell and to set up some basic healthcare guidelines for all of them.

Getting there was no ordeal for it is located centrally. The campus is larger than I expected and has a kitchen garden in addition to a small playing field. Girls, small and big, tall and short, fair and dark seem to be all over the place giggling, talking and creating a noise in general. The atmosphere is happy. They have no formal office for me so I have been given the wardens room for my consultation. My first patient is a girl around nine

"What is your name?"

"Nadia" she replies

"And why do you need to see a doctor, Nadia?" I question her. This is a first for me too for we are used to seeing children accompanied by adults and I wonder if she will be here unsupervised.

"By the evening my legs really hurt", she says to me "Here" holding on the her calves and rubbing them

Examining her I find nothing the matter with her, so I use this opportunity to question her about this facility

"Do you have dormitories?" I ask her

"Yes there are twelve of us in a dormitory and we have a sister-mother who supervises us", she answers, having no inhibitions about divulging any details."

"What is a sister-mother?" I want to know

"The girls who grow up here are asked what they wish to do when they finish school. If by then they wish to study further then that is arranged. But if they want to stay for more time, or find a small job then they have to contribute to the care of the younger ones. Every sister-mother has ten girls in her charge and she is responsible for our care, studies and to look after us. She will listen to our problems and solve them"

"Are you happy Nadia?"

"Yes, doctor Aunty, I am happy"

Finishing my exam I decide she has 'growing pains' which are common in this age group.

I see several girls and mostly they just have minor issues and are a happy and communicative lot, seeming to be secure in their new home and comfortable with their mother-sister arrangements.

Leaving I meet up with Mr. and Mrs. Naidu and congratulate them on this venture.

These semi medical visits to 'Parivartan' became my routine and to my surprise I enjoyed them thoroughly for as I got familiar with them the girls would just drop by for a chat and an informal counseling session.

One sometimes finds happiness where one least expects it.

Another silly notion hits the dust.

It restored my faith in human nature in a way. I enjoy going there and contrary to my expectations it makes me appreciate the sheer optimism of human nature for these girls are happy with a balanced and optimistic view of life and thankful for the chance they have been given by fate.

My work has many dimensions and in this context I have to go to Switzerland, a busman's holiday as I have a conference to attend. But this time I have promised myself two days exclusively for myself. Last time I went I was there for four days and all of them in Geneva and I haven't even seen the famous Jungfrau. I don't think I will see it this time either. But two things that I am going to do in Switzerland this time are what Diven had once told me to do.

Sometimes I wonder if living my life in his way is strange but they are habits of a lifetime and if I wanted something different I could do it that way.

In Switzerland I want to buy myself a Swiss watch and I want to visit the Patek Philippe Museum, both of which were my late husbands recommendations. When I was last in this country I shopped for him but not for myself. For one I didn't have the money and I didn't really want anything other than chocolates, which I got, plenty of them.

So, for now, I am looking forward to the Patek Philippe Museum. My conference is in Montreux, which is a small town famous for its association with the singer Freddie Mercury whose statue is housed near the lakeshore, and in whose memory the famous Montreux Music Jazz Festival is held, which is attended by thousands of fans. Montreux is very close to Vevey, in the Canton of Vaud, which was home to Charlie Chaplin for many years.

Montreux is scenic, reaching by train after flying in the country is cool and green, the air fragrant with the scent of flowers carrying secrets across the waters of the Lake Genève. After the heat of Delhi this is heaven. Sitting in a lakeside restaurant with a friend for dinner I think of Diven and hope that someday, maybe in another life we can be here together.

I have learned not to disbelieve, there is so much more to the universe than our limited knowledge of it.

Conferences are great levelers. You meet doctors from across the globe and sometimes make unusual friendships. I met Fatima, who is from Malaysia and who is also on her own. It seemed natural to tie up for sight seeing and we visited the Chateau de Chillon together. This Chateau is the most famous landmark in this part of the world visible from miles on either side of the lake. It is a huge stone fortress built as early as the tenth century and was home to the Counts of Savoy in the twelfth century. Possibly gained popularity after being featured in one of Byron's works 'The Prisoner of Chillon' which is a poem based on Francois de Bolevard who was a monk imprisoned in this chateau.

The Chateau de Chillon is a popular tourist attraction. It has dungeons with chains and fetters and an old wood guillotine. All in all it has an old world charm that plays on the senses and takes the mind to a day and age long gone. The original bedchamber and a birthing chamber can make your hair stand on end, they are so primitive and eerie, cold and gloomy too.

Looking at this place one can see the contrasts, a guillotine and a birthing chamber, death and life side by side, so many other things must coexist, each necessary for the other to have any meaning, darkness and light, joy and sorrow, night and day, beauty and ugliness, good and evil. For without one the other is incomprehensible. Sorrow is a part of life and grief must be accepted.

Wandering around here I think of my husband as always and wish he were here with me. I can no longer use the term grieving for I am no longer in grief, more like a sadness which has become a part of me, just wistful sometimes and sweet. But in all honesty the pain is much less, like a wound that is starting to heal and so on that accounts it hurts sometimes.

This has come about very slowly but not without effort. Effort to look at the good in life and work at eliminating negativity.

This castle has been here for centuries and must have been witness to so much; if walls could talk they would relate some chilling tales.

Meeting Fatima in Montreux was interesting too. She belongs to Malaysia and when she talks about her life I get the impression that there are many more restraints in her life in spite of being a doctor than exist in India. For one, she has little or no say in financial decisions she says and that in spite of being educated and working. Maybe the females in India are not given a bad deal comparatively but we just need more education in our country, for both the sexes.

I do have on my agenda the Swiss watch I am planning to buy. In all places in this country from train stations to public market places you see the most amazing clocks. Names like Baume and Mercier, Raymond Weil, Tissot are common. I am absolutely loving this. Huge clocks at railway stations and the stations too are a pleasure, so few people and so clean.

I miss my India, the noise, the bustle of people and the liveliness.

As to my buying, well, that I planned to do in Geneva, but have decided to check Montreux as well. There are shops selling watches in every corner of Switzerland. Finally I choose to go to a store in Montreux and decide on a Longines Conquest a simple watch no bling or gold in it and elegant.

I have kept a promise to my husband, to wear a good watch.

This means a lot to me and I hope he can see me wherever he is.

How could I not but cry doing this? I wear my new watch, come out, and sit in a public park and cry. But these tears today are not so much of grief as of reminiscence, a feeling of going back and missing and of reliving moments with him.

Looking at my watch and thinking of all the things which we had wanted to do together and which I will now do alone.

For do them I will, all the things he had wanted me to do.

And the things, which can only be done together, they will have to wait.

For another lifetime, of the seven he has promised to me.

LIFE HAS CHANGED

*"Light is filtering in
there is a crack in my shell"*

The human psyche is complex. There is a capacity for immense fortitude and yet the mind can be weak so often. Capable of sinking into the depths of human depravity and darkness and finding solace in violence, drugs and alcohol we are also capable of forsaking all this and rising to the heights of artistic creation, music and touching the stars.

What is it that makes great men? Are they born that way or do circumstances shape them?

Possibly it is a combination of environmental factors, some intrinsic capability, with opportunity and luck thrown in for good measure. But one factor in unarguable and that is faith whether it is in one's own abilities or in 'Kismet' for faith can move mountains and can make things 'happen'

When studying medicine we are taught that we utilize about twenty percent of our brain. Which could be interpreted as meaning that we are capable of a great deal more than we do.

We create our own limitations and then let them tie us to a life of the mundane and ordinary. To be able to break the shackles of the inane and head to the special needs a stimulus. Great poetry is sometimes composed after heartbreak and sorrow. We weave fantasies, for there will be many things which one will do some day, dreams which will be indulged when the time is right and some secret ambitions which will never be voiced for fear of being ridiculed.

Why not now?
Why don't we do what we want to do NOW?

For 'now' we are busy doing what is expected of us, the routine which is grilled into us from childhood, the normal life. Well I have started thinking that I will do what I want to do now and if its silly or stupid, then so be it.

If you were to put 'Salsa' on 'You Tube' you could find some grannies doing the salsa and why not, they are having a good time and aren't hurting anyone. Unfortunately all this highflying thinking doesn't always translate into action. But thinking is the first step and only then can doing possibly become the next. Many great events in the world most probably started, as someone's daydreams and maybe mine will too.

Well, I have now, and I am going to work on it. Yesterday is gone and with it a lot of the baggage we carry around in our minds, tomorrow is ephemeral and misty with potential but with no certainty that we will even see it. But 'now' is here and so I am going to do with it all the things which I want to do and not leave it for later or for tomorrow.

I am looking for change in my life.

Sometimes one should be careful what one wishes for. For when it happens it may just not be what you wanted. It's a moment, a mood, a edginess which leads one into looking. My heart is a bit lighter now and its as though I have learned to live with my grief, to heal a little and want to now get ahead of it.

The aim of all this is not to forget, for that is not possible, but to let my past be a part of me and to try to let go of the pain so I can see to the future. This didn't happen automatically but because I have decided that my life is precious, to waste it is criminal and I want more than to let it drift by. Time has slowly but surely helped to heal some of the hurt, and now I can think of my sweetheart without tears and heartbreak. There is still a lot of sadness but with it, to temper the pain, there is an acceptance.

Letting go is also disheartening; we cling to grief in our minds. It preoccupies us and fills our mind. When you start letting it go there is emptiness in your mind, maybe not unpleasant but empty all the same.

Time to fill the emptiness.

I want grow flowers. The thought of planting something and watching it grow is satisfying. But I don't know much about flowers and don't have much space to grow them either. One could go in for the potted plants I'm sure but it wouldn't be much fun. Should I get seeds or saplings? Whatever I do get it will have to be saved from Merlin for he is often destructive these days. As a puppy he was so good but now it is not unusual to walk into the house and find a cushion he has chewed or a book he has reduced to tatters.

Don't know whether to beat him or pamper him.

It came to a head finally one night. I am on call on certain days of the week, which means if some patient is admitted into the PICU who needs immediate attention I have to go and see it. It doesn't happen often but when it does its tiring for having done with the days work it is taxing to head off to hospital again at night. This eventful night heading back home close to midnight, and thinking of my cozy bed and sleep with pleasure, I approach the house after parking my car pausing to notice that the window has a funny whitish look similar to snow.

Nothing registers particularly for I am bone tired.

Then I open the door and find myself in a room, which looks like it has been ransacked; with cushions on the floor and this white shadow, which I was seeing, is the stuffing of the sofa, the synthetic down or cotton filling. It covers the floor of the living room and Merlin cowers in the corner fully aware that he has done something wrong.

I saw red. My precious leather sofa, ripped in the middle, ruined.

Before I can stop and think I react. I open the door and go out and get the stick, which I sometimes carry when I walk him and I, start beating him up.

"Useless idiotic animal. Stupid dog. I fed you before I left and walked you and this is what you have done"

I hit him with the stick till he ran towards the door and then I opened the door and kicked him out into the yard and closed the door.

"Let him stay out tonight. I am not going to let him into the house and maybe tomorrow I will go and give him to someone who will have him".

I made myself a cup of tea and surveyed the damage. After I have put all the stuffing back it doesn't look all that bad. Its ruined but then . . ..

I put my ear to the door and listen.

There is no sound from outside.

What if Merlin has run away? But no there is a door leading out, its bolted and he can't open it.

Why can't I hear him? He must be scared there, on his own in the dark.

No I am not going to let him in.

I went to my room and lay down. But I can't sleep and I wonder if I have I hurt him a lot?

"Oh God maybe I've broken his leg or something that's why he hasn't come up and made a noise".

I steal out to check and find that he is sitting under the stairs and just when I go out he creeps up, tail between his legs, head resting on his outstretched paws, waiting.

He sees me and whines.

He looks so woebegone my heart melts.

What am I to do, I feel like hugging him, but I can't do that, he is in the doghouse. I love my Merlin so much but then why does he do things like this, so destructive, and stupid.

Can't leave him out alone all night.

I let him back into the house. He heads to a corner and stands there, a tentative wag, waiting

Finally I give in,

"Come in and sleep Merlin"

What do I do with him? I really don't know. He is in the house the whole day and so good. But if I go out in the evening I can expect damage. Maybe he is scared on his own after dark even though I leave the lights burning. I still haven't figured it out why but I have got a solution for the time being which though I don't like I still do.

If I go out in the evening I tie Merlin on a leash inside the house clear of any furniture. I hate to do it but then I don't want to resort to beating him again.

My sofa though mended was never the same again and finally when Merlin was a bit older we changed it. Older because then I hope he will not go for the new one.

Big and small he did destroy things off and on but I think after that episode I got careful and accepted that he will improve as he gets older.

For other than that episode Merlin is now a great pet. He walks with discipline and behaves well.

But Sangeeta has some strange concerns where he is concerned

'Bhabhiji?'She says one evening 'have you noticed something about Merlin?'

"What?" I ask her

"You know, you know", pausing as if looking for the right words and then continuing "when we look at dogs from the back you can make out whether it is a male or a female dog. With Merlin there is nothing"

This is something I have noticed too. He doesn't seem to have anything really to show for a male dog. Trust Sangeeta to comment on this and then before I can reply she continues

"And when I take him for a walk, if he ever sniffs at another dog, it's a dog. "Pause "dog, you know, a boy dog"

Waiting for me to say something and as I am quiet she emphasizes her point

"A dog you know, never a" pause again

"Female dog, bitch" I supply

"Yes always a dog. Do you think Merlin is 'gay'?"

I kept on staring at her, and then I laughed.

"Sangeeta, don't be silly"

But Sangeeta is serious. I don't believe this.

"How does it matter?" I ask her "even if he is"

She doesn't have an answer to that one but still we fix to see the vet to figure if all is well. Calling to fix an appointment I find that there is a new vet in the office. So much the better I think to myself.

We are given a time the next evening and we both walk our baby to the doctors. Once there he is weighed and measured. His weight is Twenty-five Kilograms, no wonder he seems big.

This new vet, he isn't impressed

"What are you feeding him?" he asks me

A bit unnerved for I can sense the criticism I reply carefully

"I feed him twice a day. In the morning he has the dog food "Pedigree" and in the evening I give him either meat, eggs or cottage cheese with bread or Roti. And other than that he eats everything that is cooked in the house, like the veggies, cabbage, carrots, tomatoes. . . ." I trail off as I see his incredulous look

"You feed the dog tomatoes?" he comments as though it is an offense

"No I mean he eats a tomato or two" I am definitely floundering now

"And the eggs you give, with the yolk I presume?" he is definitely not pleased, I can tell

"Labs have a tendency to get fat and they are prone to arthritis of the hips. Your dog is overweight and will soon be obese at this rate. I will give you a diet chart. Please follow it".

He continues, "Have you given him Vitamin D?"

"Er, No, nobody told me to' "I try to tell him about Merlin's problem with delayed adolescence but somehow he is not in a mood to listen. And this vitamin D thing, what is this I want to ask, both the dog and me are D deficient are we?

Merlin gets his shots and we leave, none the wiser. Seems to me that getting along with vets is difficult for me.

We, as Pediatricians, deal with our patients and their parents with so much care and concern, handling them with kid gloves and never overtly critical of parenting techniques, markedly gentle and subtle in our advise and here I am taking so much bullshit from this jerk.

The vet could certainly learn from us.

Sangeeta is not impressed with the way I have conducted myself on this occasion and does not hesitate to say so

'You are such a big doctor and you let him say all that to you. You could have made him shut up. Merlin is nice and healthy. He is just scaring you to sell his medicines'

Possibly. Possibly, but then. . . ..

Oh well what can one do about that. Maybe we are feeding the dog wrong. It's just that most of the times Merlin is a family member and he eats what I do. Best forgotten, my visits to the vet.

Back, to the flower business, or the planting of them.

There are these mobile gardeners for I don't know what else to call them, who go around the place on bicycles, which have carts behind them, full of plants and flowers. I have seen them especially on Sundays and they sell saplings. I could buy them, it would be simpler than going hunting on my own and I could get this person whom I buy from to check on them from time to time for a small fee I think.

So I call for one of these when I see him cycling in the area carrying an array, which can make the eyes glad. Flowers in small pots all colors purple, reds, pink, white and leafy plants to which I cannot give a name. I tell Sangeeta to help me choose. There are dahlias which I am told are sturdy and will plant easily and marigolds and azaleas. The rose bushes, small with the thorns don't seem very impressive but he assures us they will bloom with time and care. So finally we take dahlias in three colors purple, pink and red and the rose bushes. The azaleas are potted and a lovely peach color. We choose to have the clusters of flowers around the 'Tulsi' plant, which is in the center. The dahlias go on either side, as do the sweet Williams and the azaleas, which come potted.

Finally, a rose bush in one corner.

The other corner is still bare and for this he suggests a banana tree which when I look at it is just a small plant with two leaves. I am told they grow very wide trunks and will it be able to grow in this small space I wonder. The gardener Mr. Amar Singh is helpful saying that it is slow but will definitely grow. A banana tree, oh wow wow in my front yard I can hardly wait to see it grow. Finally giving us instructions on the care of the plants he leaves telling us he will be back in two weeks time to check on them.

After he goes I stand on the verandah and look at the plants, they are so pleasing to the eye though the flowers are only few yet the thought of the rose bush flowering appeals. Will it?

Merlin now loose after the man has gone tries his best to eat the dahlias getting several whacks in the bargain and settling for chewing some leaves which have fallen off.

I can see the plants have caught his interest, which means we have to be extra careful. The banana plant is rather ugly and doesn't look impressive at all.

I hope it doesn't all kind of fade off but there isn't much else to do but wait. Growing things is an effort of patience and I doubt if I could do it from the seeds. These only need water and some sunlight and we can manage them.

And of course they need protection from Merlin.

Work has been the same as it always but I am aware of some disenchantment, which doesn't seem to be going away. Medicine is a demanding mistress and up until now I have been a slave to it, dedicated and satisfied. Of late, there are times when I find myself a bit short on patience with my patients and not just that I am not empathic. It also seems as though work now percolates into every aspect of life leaving no privacy at all. I get X-rays on whats app, videos of crying kids with a concern of seizures, pictures of rashes and even kids poop and requests for prescriptions. Putting a

"No professional consultations on whats app please"

Does not seem to have helped for they continue all the same. I am a bit tired of blocking of numbers. I may just delete it but I like getting pics from various friends and Kiya is fond of using it too. Knowing as I do the demands of my work I can also comprehend that the change in my personal circumstances is likely to increase the stress of my work but so far it has been my escape and now this constant, persistent, low-grade irritation is worrying.

I decide to take a day or two off in the middle of the week and spend some lazy time or just go visit my Dad for he stays out of town.

On my day off I have a lazy breakfast with Sangeeta humming happily in the kitchen. I sit at the dining table with the dog sleeping at my feet and I admire the flowers, which I can see through the window.

A feeling of satisfaction fills me,
"Tweet, tweet"
That's my phone.

A message on whats app. The new whiz app for social networking and it pings so often that I have now put different sounds for the messaging and whats app. The message comes with a 'beep, beep' and whats app with this bird like tweety sound.

The color of the light is also different, cyan for whatsapp; I liked this color, bluey actually.

I check the message and since I am not wearing my glasses which I have recently acquired for reading I see just a pic, maybe a book cover or a cartoon and a

"Hi"

It's only a number, no name.

Crank, I think, or a patient. I am about to delete it when something holds my attention.

I know this number, for it seems familiar.

But if I know it why isn't it saved on my phone? That's unusual for I never remember numbers these days. There is no need to and since you save them by name you don't get to see them half the time.

Why does this number seem familiar?

It comes to me . . . A long time ago.. Receiving messages from this number

"You should wear saris more often, they suit you"

"Bright and beautiful" And some equally complimentary messages.

Mohit.

Doing a rewind in my mind I go back to what I am remembering.

Dr. Mohit Sivakaran is a gastroenterologist who used to work in our hospital some five or six years ago. I don't recall when I have last seen him and my last memory is that of seeing him in the emergency department and his telling me something about a publication in a journal. He had been sending me some messages off and on, rather complimentary and had once asked me out for lunch.

Other than that I have never had any interaction with him. And the reason that number was not saved was because at that time the messages were a source of irritation for me. I was happily married and had no time or wish for some silly dalliance.

That was many years ago, many light years ago.

Like a different lifetime, it now seems.

I try to recall more details but my memory is blurry. A tall, big built man, a bit overweight but well proportioned, greying hair and no glasses. Can't recall more than that. Don't remember seeing him in any social function in the hospital and the hospital has plenty of those, annual dinners, parties for various festivals and many get togethers for all reasons. I had never met him in any.

I put on my glasses to check the message properly. It's a book cover, Dr. Mohit has written a book.

Wondering how I should reply I message

"?? Hi"

Does this seem rude, not to me, it's longer than his message anyway

"We should meet sometime" he messages back

"Ok" that's me without paying much attention.

I go back to my daydreaming and plan going over to my Dads. Dad's birthday is around the corner and maybe I can take him out for a meal.

'Tweet, tweet' that's my phone again.

"Lunch today?" That's the message on whats app from Dr. Mohit.

I look at this message, and as usual think of fate and kismet for this, not the message but the timing for it's an amazing coincidence. I have the day off today or else I never am available for lunch on a working day. Not giving myself time for a rethink I message back

"Ok, where?"

Hardly a gracious reply but it is simplified by Mohit calling. We exchange pleasantries and then decide to meet up at a popular restaurant in the vicinity of my workplace. Possibly he is under the impression that I am going to come from work. Can't blame him for that one.

Giving myself no time to think I tell Sangeeta that I am going for a shower. I am going out for lunch for I am well aware that if I let myself think even for a minute this lunch will be off.

Dressing up and driving to meet him I make an effort to recall what little I do know about him. A common friend had told me, six years ago, that Mohit was going through a rough time, divorce proceedings. That has stayed with me for though

I don't know his status now I would prefer not to go out with a married man. Don't know for sure though, six years is a long time and he could be married again for all I know.

Making a point to myself I have dressed very casually for this is not a date. What is it, this sudden impulsiveness, going out now when for weeks on end I don't meet even Dad, Kiya or my sister?

Just a desire for change, for something new.

Possibly setting myself up for a big disappointment. The lunch venue is a fancy hotel with a nice buffet lunch. We meet and greet each other a bit self consciously for we don't know each other well and then its been a long time since we met.

Lunch was a bit of a stilted and constrained affair with talk largely centering on work and medicine and other generalities. A testing of waters I think, a bit amused at myself. Mohit looks the same, a bit greyer, a bit older. I must be looking like hell compared to the last time he has seen me but he is too polite to say so. As I fill my plate with meat and mayonnaise I see him favor lots of greens and vegetables.

"Are you vegetarian?" I question, for that would be really sad as I love my meat and cannot imagine eating out for vegetarian food. What a waste

"No" he replies "though we do not cook meat in the house"

Each to his own, I guess.

This is something, which is common in our country though I fail to truly understand it. You can eat meat but not in your own house, you can drink but not in your own house. Traditions and old customs die hard in our country and vegetarianism is one of them. Not my business, not my circus, not my monkeys.

I do know he had left our hospital but am unaware of his present workplace and I ask him

"Where are you working now?"

"After leaving Karma Hospital I joined the Max group but that was not a great experience and so I finally was working at the Modern Clinic. I have quit there a few months ago and now I am going to two or three clinics. Something like freelancing"

Suddenly, strangely I find myself envying him. I have been working in my hospital for over ten years and though there are times when it palls, I couldn't even in my wildest dreams think of just walking out. He has changed three hospitals in six years, takes a lot of guts or just stupidity and I don't know as yet where he fits.

For all this I find Mohit a very pleasant companion. He is unfailingly polite and conversation is comfortable. Finishing lunch which I end with a scrumptious selection of pastries, from which he refrains we leave our table and stroll out.

"We must do this again" Mohit says

"Definitely. Its been nice meeting you, thank you for a lovely lunch" I reply

Well some answers I do have now. Partly the curiosity of meeting someone out of my normal small circle and part of it because it's a man.

How long has it been since I indulged in a small intimate dinner, some wine and pleasant conversation with a man? Just forever and possibly its something you miss without even realizing it and do I need to lay down some rules for it, for myself and for him?

The dating game, that's what it is called. I had never been part of this game I think for when I met my husband he was the first man I truly got close to. And because I met him so early in my life and considered myself committed the years when girls play these games didn't work that way for me. In medical school, where one may or may not form companionships which are in for the long run, was a time when I focused only on my studies, work and more studies. And soon after becoming a doctor I got married. And that was my life.

Kiya got married very young for her family found a good match for her. She wasn't even eighteen and married and at twenty she was the mother of two. This is not uncommon in our country though all this is slowly coming to meet with rebellion from the girls. Young girls who only one generation ago in India often nursed no greater ambition than getting 'a good match' now want much more out of life. They want to study and have a career and then get married. We have been Americanized in many ways, which are subtle. During my medical school days when Kiya was already married I wondered if she had missed out on a part of her youth, the growing up, the awareness, the flirting and the fun which is part of the teenage years. She had always seemed happy with her life.

Now I feel like that too, wondering if I am part of this big singles game, which I do not know how to play, and am not sure I want to be a part of. But it tempts, and it's good for the ego.

I am not sure Mohit will call again.

My work has been a source of dissatisfaction for me lately for I find myself at odds sometimes with my colleagues. A kind of disenchantment with medicine is setting in. Over the years the practice of medicine has changed. Having watched my parents, who are both doctors, in practice I can see the change all around me. Medicine is slowly becoming a business, not a vocation and the patient is the consumer, the client, demanding, suspicious and often ungrateful. Many doctors start to feel like this after long years of work. The emotional rewards are poor and the commitment high. I think it starts to take its toll. This has been on my mind off and on for some time and it's a sign of a mind looking for change.

Feeling moody and unsettled I think of Diven and remember his saying about our retirement

'We will grow flowers and vegetables and watch them grow. You can work at a slower pace maybe three to four hours a day and the rest of the time we can just chill, listen to music and watch movies. And see the world'

With him around it had seemed possible to start planning for a change but losing him made me cling to the familiar, my work and hospital as the anchor for my life.

But now there are times when my anchor feels like a noose around my neck, slowly tightening and stifling me.

Mohit is responsible for this avalanche of thoughts in my mind. For the way he is working is something few doctors ever do, it is too unstable and income wise possibly very labile. I didn't know him well enough to question the chain of events leading to this but it seems adventurous, risky, somewhat foolish too after such a long effort. We are like well programmed laboratory rats, to work hard and harder, and different is not allowed.

I call Kiya and tell her 'Hi fats, howz life with you? Guess what.. I had gone out for lunch with somebody"

"I hope he is not married" Kiya's responses are sometimes so predictable.

"No, that he is not" I say and then proceed to gamely answer her barrage of questions, which range from personal too ridiculous.

"Doesn't have a steady job?" I can hear her thoughts though she doesn't voice them, there are you steady as a rock and this person is he flighty and irresponsible.

She should have said deadly dull, boring and predictable for me. All are true.

"Does he have any kids?"

"I don't know Kiya; don't make a mountain out of a molehill. I may never see him again for all you know"

"Hmmmm. . . . Keep me updated"

I want to tell Kiya about my work and the issues there but I know this is something she doesn't really understand. So I sound out my father when we go out for dinner

"Dad these days I am often out of sorts at work" I say to him after we have both had a drink or two and mellowed out a bit.

'Take up a hobby, go out more and keep another dog or cat if it appeals to you"

There is no point in this conversation. I can understand what he means and also understand the way he feels. He worries about me, he is old and now sometimes he seems frail, and I don't want to burden him with all this. Maybe work problems should be tolerated and lived with.

Things sometimes click at the oddest of times. For me understanding came on hearing some nasty gossip about some common friends. Kiya called me, her mood somber and upset "I don't know what the world is coming to these days. Its absolutely scandalous. Sita has walked out on her husband. Suddenly. Without a word of explanation. With both the kids. I met them only a few days back at a party and they were fine then. Sahil is devastated. I wonder what happened?"

"*No*", I think, "*nothing happened suddenly*". I don't know these people very well but I have an insight into this situation. It must have built up over years and then come to a boil. Turned unbearable and led to this difficult decision on Sita's part. For some reason I equate this to my work situation, things are building up there too and I am living with them. Maybe tolerance isn't all that great for if you go on stretching something all the time its bound to give in sooner or later. That could be your mind or your patience, whichever.

Prior to his illness I had already started to formulate a plan for a smaller practice, outpatient based rather than hospital based. But before any of my half-baked plans could see the light of day Diven had this disease. From then on it became the center point of our lives wiping out any other concern and carrying us in its wake. Had he lived would I still have been so dissatisfied with my work? Probably not for then the continuing treatment and follow-ups would mandate my hospital attachment. But now suddenly it doesn't seem so important.

Mohit messaged on whats app and sent some pictures. Flowers, pretty pictures, scenic shots of various parts of the world. We kept in touch for a few days and then he invited me out again.

This time I am going to be going knowing what I am starting even if it's tentative. Thinking again I remember the advice I had dished out to Sara so blithely

"No harm in going out. Going out is not a commitment" I don't need to beat myself with that stick over and over again.

I have a date, I think.

MERLIN IS TWO

"My companion, my shadow
My friend, Merlin"

It's been a long long day. Came in at five and then a trauma transport call and had to go back at seven and now its close to ten. Tired and irritated as I enter the house something catches my attention. A glint of gold? Ye.es. There seems to be a fancy envelope in my mailbox. Opening the mailbox and picking it up I realize it's a wedding invitation. Gilded edges and a picture of the God Ganesha on the front with fine golden strings for decoration. And the upper left hand corner reads, 'Vikrant weds Misha'

Vikrant? I think to myself, that tall gangly teenager with the irritating voice. I am only ten years off mark I realize when I count the years. A long time ago it seems now, when I worked in a smaller hospital the staff often lived on campus and so families had a chance to get acquainted and make small social circles. I recall having; 'Kitty parties' with a group of ten consultant families and the rules were simple, you had to have it in your own house and cook if you could or just call everyone to get something edible, potluck. The children were included and these parties invariably ended with silly games and a lot of juvenile, if drunk, good humor. Vikrant is DM's son, the doctor I had consulted for myself and I know he had joined medical school. I guess he is old enough to be married now and the girl must be one of his own choice as the name is unusual and does not seem to belong to his community.

I pull myself up; certain things are unfortunately ingrained in us. Religion, caste systems, states, regions, families, horoscopes all matter in matrimonial affairs. It's been a long time since I attended a wedding and Indian weddings are hugely elaborate affairs, which go on for days. I have been invited for two functions, the wedding ceremony and the 'Mehendi'. The mehendi is a function from the girl's family on the day of the application of Henna to the bride's hands and feet. This is done to the accompaniment of much singing and dancing by her friends and is often a popular occasion for match making in the traditional Indian wedding.

I would like to go and meet up with everybody for a lot of my old colleagues and friends will be their and its time to catch up with life.

Musing to myself, I look at Merlin sleeping at the foot of my bed. He has long since made his own rules about where he sleeps, what he eats, when and where he goes for a walk. Any attempt to get him to sleep in a doggie bed was futile from when he was six months old for he chewed them to bits and slept at the foot of my bed. And then as he got older he jumped on the bed and his whining and moaning on being displaced made me accept his demands.

Like the Arab and the camel somewhat.

Now he sleeps at the foot end, on or off the bed as per his own wishes. Sometimes I think.

Every day is my dog's day.

My doggie is going to be two years old. Looking at him I think back to when I decided to get him and thank my stars that I did.

Merlin can sense my moods and if I am low I will find him at my feet with no fuss and no bad behavior at all. He walks with discipline and follows most commands. And yes, now he looks like a male dog. He weighs thirty kg and is a potent deterrent to any burglar. Little would any would be robber know that Merlin loves everybody and would likely welcome even a thief. He is playful and tends to jump on people if very excited. Ah well.. That hasn't made us popular at all. The other day my neighbor returned from her grocery shopping and putting down her bags to take out her keys found herself greeted by my dog putting both his paws on her shoulders. Her scream made him cower in fright. So much for my big watchdog, sometimes he is even scared of the cat next door.

Now for his birthday I think I will get him a doggie cake. I have heard they make them at 'head over tails' some website for pets. It's definitely something to celebrate for he is my companion and my friend ever so reliable, loving and loyal.

So what if he still chews shoes at any given opportunity. He has rules for this too you know. If he chews up one shoe of a pair and practically mangles it and you give him the second one of the same pair in sheer frustration, he will not touch it. Only one from each pair he can lay his paws on. After that he loses interest.

My mind still on Vikrant's forthcoming wedding and the kid as I had last seen him. I recall an incident which had taken place during one of these silly kitty parties. As often happens towards the end of an evening the men had holed up together leaving the women and the children to their own games.

Getting ready to leave I was caught by DM who is grinning foolishly and he says to me "Your husband is a lucky man, doc"

"Why? Because he is married to me," I laugh back at him

"No, that's not how it goes. It's more complicated than that"

And seeing that he means to tell me I wait for him to continue and he goes on

"We were all discussing our days, schedules and what we consider high points in the day and for most of us it came down to when we sit down to a drink in the evening or when we start a game of golf in the morning" As he pauses I wonder if Diven has said something silly for we are all pleasantly high at this point. And he continues asking me "Do you want to know what your husband said?"

"What did he say?" I ask the question he expects, crossing my fingers behind my back for Diven is amazing for the occasional faux pas if inebriated

"He said" again a long pause

"Oh finish what you are saying for Gods sake DM", I'm getting irritated now

"Well Diven said 'I get home before she does and the high point of my day is when she walks into the house and says "Baby, I'm home"'. Any man who can still feel like that after ten years of marriage is a truly lucky man"

Yes, he may have a point there, I think we had been fortunate for we hadn't felt the boredom many marriages see as they go along and Diven had been consistently fixated on me to the point of being very possessive at times. Possibly because we didn't have children and so tended to focus on each other.

Also makes you miss someone that much more when they're gone.

Going for this wedding I will be meeting all these friends again after a long time and now without him. I smile, and think, I must not let him down in that case.

I think I will buy a new sari for this wedding, a beautiful Indian silk; maybe a 'kanjeevaram'. The sari is a dress, which comes in all avatars. Cottons, chiffons, silks and every color under the sun, with borders and spangles and sequins too these days. But the traditional silks have a grace which is timeless. 'Kanjeevaram' silks are the traditional weaves from south India and are very beautiful and ethnic. And I have a great fondness for them.

Also though I have been out for lunch once more with Mohit, casually dressed, I think the next time I will wear a sari. It's more formal and makes a statement of sorts.

Going out with Mohit, the second time, I was somewhat more comfortable and contrary to our first meeting, am willing to find fault with everything. He chooses to order without consulting me and though he orders fish, which I do like I wish he had asked. Something similar to saying

"We should meet" instead of

"Would you like to meet?"

Maybe a fine difference but when you're nitpicking its important. Then, he just like Kiya has some strange notions about eating healthy and presumably assuming my acceptance refuses the dessert.

"Has it got something to do with being overweight" I wonder about this preoccupation with eating healthy, for it doesn't seem to have done either Kiya or him any good.

For me a meal is incomplete without a sweet to end it. Leaving after having lunch with Mohit, I went to the closest outlet of Dunkin Donuts and ordered two doughnuts, one strawberry delight and one mandarin orange, and sat and munched them happily. So very unhealthy and so satisfying!!

My mind rebels, maybe I am being unreasonable. I find him pleasant and easy to talk to. Sometimes these days we speak to each other in the evening too giving a rundown of the day that was. Its nice having someone to complain to about my grouses against my work. He is a good listener, patient and doesn't interrupt me when I take off on a tirade. I think I just need to give this new friendship some time to evolve as it will.

Mohit is very fond of sending pictures on the phone via whatsapp and now I am getting used to getting some pictures of flowers and jokes too. That is how it works in the modern world and possibly I belong to the old fashioned lot for I find it entertaining on occasion but certainly would not go down as my idea of romance.

I think at seventeen it is very easy to like someone and even to fall in love, for youth is like a clean slate, innocent of fixed notions and bias. Getting on to fifty one is fussy, inclined to find fault and be very discerning. I have a tendency to fault finding which I need to put on hold.

And so saying I decide to go sari shopping with of course, Kiya. As we wander through this huge sari store, which could cater to any taste, pocket or social occasion I find that for once the tables have turned. I am choosing the more sedate, less flamboyant and understated saris while Kiya is going towards the reds and the golds.

"I thought you wanted to buy something for a wedding" Kiya says as I reach out for a particularly pretty grey and white sari.

"Yes I do, but I don't want any gold and I don't want reds," I tell her.

"You can't wear grey to a wedding" I am reprimanded as she leads me to a particularly bright purple and mustard combination and then seeing the distaste on my face she continues

"What is wrong with you? I thought you liked bright colors."

"Nothing is wrong with me. I like bright colors but I like my saris graceful. I will buy saris for a wedding but I want the kind that I can finally wear to conferences and to give my lectures and gaudy doesn't work too well there"

I know Kiya is a bit out of sorts for she is worrying about her daughter. Alisha, Kiya's daughter, married now but still a baby in our eyes has been having some health problems and Kiya is concerned about her. I do not wish to add to her worries and I know she is seeing some pretty dreams about my future and I don't want to disillusion her. Hence her preoccupation with bright and colorful saris for me. We finally settle for a beautiful autumn hued sari with the yellow border and another in a muted purple.

As is usual for us following shopping sprees we go to the patisserie for some coffee and cakes or pastries. Kiya is on a perpetual diet, which she apparently reneges on only when she is with me or so I am told.

"How is your diet coming along these days, Kiya?"

She looks at me suspiciously suspecting that I am taking a dig at her, which is the norm. As far back as I can remember she is counting calories and eating all kinds of weird items in the name of health food. These days it is raw papaya and flax seed, earlier it was greens and meals, which had to have boiled vegetables. As I listen to her I make the mistake of saying

"Mohit is also largely vegetarian. I think he only ends up eating chicken when he takes me out for a meal" I realize I have given her the best topic to take her mind of her own problems but by then it is too late

"Hey, do you have any picture of him? Show me for I want to see what he looks like"

I do have pictures of him, which he has sent me recently, some old one and a few fairly recent. It is somehow important for him to meet with Kiya's approval though I reiterate my point that I may not end up seeing him for long.

How do I get this across to her? She is not in a mood to understand for as she sees the pictures she pronounces, "He is nice. I like the way he looks". She goes on

"Now you listen to me. As we get older life tends to get lonely. It's nice to have someone to talk to, to share things with and maybe just to sit around with. Don't be judgmental, give yourself some time and give this friendship a chance"

I hear her out and want to tell her about the last time I was out with Mohit. Finishing lunch I decided to have a cup of coffee and I say so to him. He calls out to the waiter

"One cup of coffee for the lady, please"

"Wouldn't you like to have some coffee?" I question him and get the answer

"I don't drink tea or coffee" "Ok" I reply thinking about the umpteen cups of tea and coffee I consume over a normal workday and with plenty of milk and sugar.

Over my coffee I try to make him talk about himself and glean the following, he has never smoked in his life and is not much of a drinker. He watches English movies and hasn't seen a Hindi movie in about twenty odd years.

I love Hindi movies, the so-called Bollywood movies. Silly, often unrealistic with lots of songs thrown in, inane mindless romances with a healthy dose of violence. They are my idea of relaxation at the end of a long day when I don't have the energy or the concentration to read for to see a Hindi movie you don't really need much brains. Actually our movies are popular in the Middle East and other countries too for the songs and dances. Maybe not an intellectual pastime but relaxing all the same. So how does this work? If I am willing to see an English movie with him he should be willing to see a Hindi movie with me. I didn't say anything to him however. Too much too soon really.

How do I convey all this to Kiya without upsetting her? I think she has enough on her plate at present and I think I will fade out this friendship in her eyes, gently, gradually, and slowly.

So thinking I grin to myself. Interpretation by my friend "I'm glad thinking of him is making you smile" I'm glad she can't hear my thoughts.

Regards the not smoking and drinking I guess they are all the right virtues to have but these attributes are truly given a great deal of importance in India. When you say for a boy or man as is the case here "He doesn't drink or smoke" you are conveying that he is a very good person. Add "he is a pure vegetarian" and you have got saint status. Apart from that he may be a wife beater or weirdo, that wouldn't matter in the least for most part. The truth about relationships is in fact the opposite of this for we like people not so much for their perfections as for their imperfections. This maybe especially true of women for they need to feel needed and to reform the men in their lives. If the men are already perfect that would be boring.

I have always been able to talk to Kiya; she has been privy to all my emotions and dreams. But, this, what I feel these days I am unable to voice even to her. For though I am fault finding and making all kinds of excuses the fact is that somewhere, inside of me, I feel guilty. For looking down at the simple gold band on the ring finger of my left hand I accept at least in my heart the truth of my feelings. The reason why I am not comfortable with this new relationship is the fact that I feel I am married. I am committed, I am not truly willing to let him go and deep inside of me I feel this is infidelity.

Oh I am well aware of the facts, I know Diven is gone and it's been a while and I have every right to lead my life but there it is, the reality of my emotions.

Maybe I could go to a counselor and sit on the famous couch. Unlikely to go unnoticed that. So for the time I can only live with this and wait.

Saris sorted out I give the blouses for tailoring and here too I feel the generation gap. From a demure and sometimes provocative garment the blouse has gone to something with noodle straps and a minimalistic look. Imagine that, showing a great deal reminding me of the itsy bitsy yellow polka dot bikini. My tailor is an old man who has been tailoring my clothes for decades and when he sees me eying the fancy ones he says with some familiarity

"Madam should stay with the conventional look" making me wonder if this is a pick at my rather less then voluptuous contours. I wasn't planning any different.

This week it's my visit to 'Parivartan' and again I find myself enjoying this a lot more than my usual workday. Dealing with healthy children is a pleasure after the PICU where death stares one in the face so often. But the satisfaction that comes from the conviction that I may have contributed to the saving of a human life is a feeling like no other. It goes both ways, the work is tough and the rewards are high.

Maybe I am growing a bit old for it for I am convinced that intensive care should be done by the young and the very, very enthusiastic. I am better now at organizing it and do not really enjoy the hands on so much. I am forced to consider again that something is wrong in my work structure and that I need to really rethink my priorities.

Should I think of changing my job? Looking for a new one? Is that what this is all about? But I work in one of the best hospitals in the country and any other is bound to fall short in terms of facilities and equipment, which is so necessary to my line of work. But these thoughts, this restlessness buzzes repeatedly in my head, creating a whirlpool in which I drown often these days.

To change a job is not just that. It is a change of workplace and colleagues, friends. It's like moving on swampy ground, unstable after having been on terra firma for a lifetime. I don't have the nerve for it.

But over the next few days I am forced repeatedly to think about this as my tummy aches and I get repeated bouts of severe dyspepsia. Signs of stress I tell myself and drink some antacid. Possibly too much tea and coffee. But my stomach refuses to settle and many a day I feel sick looking at rich food, which I love as a rule. Increasing my dose of the horrible chalky antacid mixture I decide I will get an ultrasound if it doesn't settle in the next few days. Or a gastro consult.

Doctors are notoriously bad patients and I think we to one of the two extremes, for either we will be convinced that every twinge is the sign of a near fatal illness or we will underplay our symptoms and convince ourselves that it is nothing to worry about. Goes for me too I guess this rule for though I did have pain off and on I was reluctant to see a specialist for the first thing he'd likely ask for would be an endoscopy and I was in no mood for that. So I live with the discomfort hoping it will die a natural death.

A great deal of my work is intensive care and so with the hospitalized patients but I do a follow up and outpatients too. Usually have only two or three patients or some new referral in the OPD. Today I have an appointment for a sixteen year old, which is rather unusual for the slightly older children often end up with the internists. As is usual when a patient comes into the room either walking or in the arms of a parent one starts forming some opinion of the disease on the basis of observation even before the complaints are voiced. This child or young lady as I would call her, for she is sixteen, walks in with both parents. She looks well I think to myself, petite in her build but otherwise comfortable, no evidence of discomfort. Being an intensive care person

I rarely get the usual pediatric OPD patients but rather more of the respiratory or cardiac lot. This one looks like neither. I do know her name it is written in my appointment diary and so I start by addressing her

"Hullo Serena, I am glad you have chosen to see me. How can I help you?"

Today adolescent medicine is a line in itself, for the adolescents has a different set of problems and the teens I see are often follow-ups after hospitalization. I wait and find my patient smiling and subjecting me to an intense scrutiny. I wait for her to say something and then she puts a small photo album on my desk and says

"Doctor you don't recognize me but I have been wanting to meet you for a long time and so my parents have brought me here" She gets up from her chair and coming to my side of the desk opens up the album. It's a regular baby album and on the first page there is a picture, which shows me a tiny baby in an incubator. And on the next page..

There is a picture of me holding the tiny infant and showing it to a little girl. I look at my patient with a question on my face and she smiles, pointing her finger to the baby in the picture

"That's me" she says "And I have come to say thank you"

I look at the picture. That's me younger by sixteen years in a nursery in another hospital and that's her, the tiny baby I hold.

It would be difficult for me to put into words what I felt in that moment. She stands before me, a healthy sixteen year old and I can hardly believe it. I want to thank her for the fact that she has made this considerable effort to come and see me and for the fact that her parents have remembered my role in her life.

"I am honored to have had something to do with the fact that you are such a lovely young lady today" and find myself unable to speak for the break in my voice.

Her mother takes up "It's been a long time doctor. She was born 980 Gms and you looked after her. I have never forgotten how you always made time to talk to me, to explain and give hope. I have often spoken of you to her and on her birthday this year she said she wanted to meet you. So I brought her here"

Serena wants to click some pictures of us together again, as she puts it for 'Then' and 'Now'. I make her take a few pictures with my phone too and tell her to whatsapp me the older ones. She obliges happily. After a cursory checkup, for there is nothing the matter with her, the family leaves.

I continue my workday but my thoughts are now riveted on this incident. It is not unusual for us to have difficult saves or survivors, but for someone to come in years later is rare.

This child, this youngster, she has strengthened my faith in my profession for where else can you find this kind of satisfaction, this lasting emotional bond. No amount of money could give the kind of feeling this girl has left me with. Thank you Serena.

I am not going to give up Intensive Care. I will find a way to solve my problems and maybe take on an associate to give me some relief from the calls but I will not shift to ward work.

Once an Intensivist, always an Intensivist.

Yes, the world may have changed, and patients may have become clients. But there will always be room in medicine for the idealistic doctors and the carers, the healers. And that is what makes it worthwhile even against all the odds.

On the professional front I have now achieved so much of what I had wanted. I wish Diven were here to see it for even though a non medical person he had understood my passion for it, for practicing medicine and for teaching medicine too. I now work as part of a unit, which runs a fellowship for the pediatricians training for intensive care, and will be examiner for the fellowship too. It means reading a lot to teach the trainees. Doing medicine means you are a student for life for science advances rapidly and you have to keep pace with it.

Entering the ward I am called by one of my residents. Dr. Manish says to me

"Ma'am you have to see the baby in 3503. She is the prettiest baby I have ever seen"

This is a routine working day in the Pediatric ward and this statement from one of our doctors catches my attention in a jiffy. Manish is one of our resident doctors and a more pragmatic, down to earth, practical young man would be difficult to find. To the best of my knowledge, very little can excite him other than tennis and Roger Federer !!. And here he is, I think to myself, raving about a baby!!. And that too, practically an accolade of the highest order. A non medical person may find this a bit strange but the doctors working with babies as a part of their routine job often fail to be impressed by them as the world at large is. Babies to a Resident, or an on-duty doctor, are only often a bed number and a diagnosis.

And so I go in to have a look at Hannah. As I walk into the room I see this pretty pink and white picture in a bright yellow frock smiling happily at the world around her. Hannah sits on the hospital bed with as much aplomb as in her owns home and she seems pleased with her yet new and unfamiliar surroundings. Her dress maybe a daffodil yellow but it isn't anything as sunny as her smile for Hannah truly beams with her head tilted and her hands held out. She is a pretty package with her brown hair in a spout on her head and her eyes filled with wonder at all the new things and people around her. And I do a retake, those eyes. . . . Isn't there a slight slant to them? Oh yes there is - uh oh, Hannah is a Down.

Now this may or may not mean anything to a person reading this – a Down in medical language is a child with Downs Syndrome.

Downs is something of a truly different baby. These babies have a very distinct appearance with their very round faces and flattened back of heads, often funny misshapen low set ears, a bit of an upward slant to the eyes (because they have what is called an epicanthic fold, a fold of skin at the inner corner of the eyes) giving them a slightly oriental look which is distinctive and difficult to forget once seen. For the same reason these babies are also sometimes referred to as "mongoloid"

So when I look at Hannah the next and automatic question is
"Why is she in hospital?"

I look closely only to find that she looks pink and flushed, not just pink but maybe a bit dusky. She seems healthy, and at first glance, no sniffles and fussing that one can see. But, the fact of the matter is, Hannah has congenital heart disease and she is hospitalized to undergo surgery for the same.

And then I look at her mother, experience now giving me the foresight to look for signs of worry and stress or that hint of defensiveness that is so often a part of the parents whose who have babies with problems like this, for they are aware that their baby is unlike other babies. But here too I find no sign of any complaint against life. Hannah's mother is, like Hannah herself, smiling and happy, a pleasure to be around. So I don't probe or counsel in anyway and just attend to the baby, silently thanking her for her open and accepting attitude.

And there again comes a thought about our profession and the important roles that doctors can sometimes play in some of life's unforgettable moments. For as I can see Hannah's mother has an attitude that says that she has faith in all that is happening around her and also full faith that her child will get well. And that, believe me, leaves the onus on us and the immense responsibility to do the best by her in every way we can.

Leaving this room I feel today has definitely reestablished my faith and my commitment in my work. Yes it is taxing, and it's tiring and it is sometimes thankless but the pros are definitely more than the cons and always will be.

At the end of the day I think its all about faith, be it faith as in religion or God as the case maybe or faith in life, faith in beginnings, faith in one's own self. For as they say faith can move mountains and thinking that puts my problems in perspective.

There are times when the mind somehow moves into a negative gear and what we call anxiety prevails and you feel low. There is nothing abnormal about it and giving in to it is the worst thing one can do. Unfortunately the world today is so tuned into the quick fixes that no sooner than you worry you can have the tag of GAD or 'generalized anxiety disorder' and were it to persist for more than a few days which it would if I were to do nothing about it then you are depressed in medical terminology. Being a doctor I would be the first to agree with the consensus that a lot of the human population is consuming drugs which they do not need and which do them no good for their real or imagined ailments.

Driving my hilly route home I see there is a small new construction by the place where I had seen the peacock dance. Slowing down I realize it is a temple, a small enclosed garden with a building which has a thatched roof, unusual for our surroundings. With my present mood this seems to be a signal of sorts for I feel that I am being beckoned to go there.

How long has it been since I visited a temple? Though not religious in the strictest sense of the world I can recall even as a child, holding my mothers hand and going to the temple. Simple rituals, taking flowers from the flower seller outside the temple and getting the sweet from the priest after praying are norm for all the children in this country I am sure. Thursday mornings were for years my time with God however I may have done it. Diven would drive me there and then he would while away time outside while I went in. I had never attempted to persuade him to go in for that has to be a desire inside of you, not something done to please anyone.

Today is Wednesday and maybe there is a signal there. I could say God is trying to tell me something but more likely it is my own mind.

The next morning I get up early, at 5 am and have a bath. I decide to walk to the temple as it is very nearby. Once there I am drawn effortlessly into a pattern, which is familiar to me over the years. I remove my slippers and give them to be put outside the building and get a token for them and them I buy the flowers and the 'prasad' which will be blessed by the priest. Entering the temple I am struck by a sense of peace and serenity which is like a balm after the self inflicted stress I have been subjecting myself to. Sitting down I close my eyes and let the refrain of the devotional hymns drift around me, playing to the background of someone playing a harmonium. My mind settles, my nerves calm down enjoying the tinkle of the bells where some child has rung them, the aroma of incense which is burning at the altar, the muted melody of people joining in to the chorus and take me to suspended moment of time, of peace and well being.

Walking out I stop for a cup of tea which is being served by a devotee for some wish which has been fulfilled and for that he is serving food in the house of God.

Heading back home I feel calmer than I have been in days, my mental discussions silenced for a while. As the day goes on I will get back to all that and maybe worry again. But for now I am at peace with myself.

A lost sheep has found its way back to the flock.

LIFE DOES GO ON

"Somewhere my love
Flowers will bloom again"

From Lara's theme 'Dr. Zhivago'

I am dying. I am having a heart attack. I was fine just ten minutes ago and then suddenly I got this severe, stabbing, intense pain in my epigastrium, which had me doubling over and clutching my upper abdomen in agony. Breaking out into a cold sweat I try to rationalize what is happening but the intensity of the pain nearly makes me pass out.

It could not have been more than five minutes though it seems more like a lifetime, and then the pain seems to shift and arc into the right side of my tummy as sharp as a knife cutting through the layers of muscle.

"*I don't want to die,*" I think to myself. "*I want to live at least for a few years*".

"*I want to go to Paris*".

"*I want to learn how to speak French*".

"I want to knit socks". I can knit pullovers but of late I have been fascinated by fancy sock knitting patterns and I want to try them out.

"I want to run in a marathon or maybe a pinkathon, the one they are having for breast cancer awareness".

There is so much I want to do yet. And . . .and . .

"My poor Merlin, who will look after him?"

Calming a bit I rationalize, the pain seems to distinctly be on the right now so its unlikely to be a heart attack. I was fine in the evening, had my dinner and now this. My appendix is out so that is not the cause. Logically that leaves me two choices as possibilities, a renal colic or a biliary colic. Attempting to straighten up I walk to my bed and try to lie down but am unable to do so for it hurts. Sitting leaning forward is bearable.

I look at the time; eleven pm. it's still not that late. I can call someone I think but then the pain seems to lessen, recede and becomes a dull ache radiating to my back. I feel mildly nauseous but nothing happens.

Should I take some medicine? I don't have much by way of painkillers in the house.

In the next few minutes the pain fades off and I feel fine. Tentatively I prod my fingers in my abdomen looking for some sign, tenderness, and a lump. Nothing.

It can only be either of the two which in inflamed or diseased, the kidney or gallbladder, I think and since I feel fine now I can get an ultrasound tomorrow morning.

The next morning I feel so well that I deliberately eat breakfast so I cannot have an ultrasound early in the morning. Midway through the day I go to Radiology and talk to Dr. Asha, an ultrasonologist. She tells me to come in for the scan. And as she runs the probe on my abdomen I watch her face not wanting to miss any ominous diagnosis.

But she is cheerful

"Well you have plenty of jewels sitting in your GB. Lots of small stones and silt"

"And?" I ask

"And" she replies "Go and see a surgeon, but from the look of it, it will have to come out"

"Doctors are so crass sometimes" I think. Being on the other side is no fun at all but then how else should she have told me?

"Is this the reason I have been having tummy aches?" I question her

She gives me a dry look, she is not a clinician and this is not her domain.

I go and fix an appointment with the nicest surgeon I know. That is Dr. Ahmad, smart and soft-spoken.

In the evening I call my Dad and tell him about the pain and he says

"Sounds like a classical biliary colic. Shouldn't be a problem. The gall bladder needs to come out. Have you decided on the surgeon as yet?"

How simple is all that? From perfectly healthy to surgery all in one day.

"I have fixed an appointment with Dr. Ahmad, Dad" I inform him and immediately

"Isn't he a bit junior?" a pause and then "If you have faith in him then its ok"

"We. .ell. . I haven't even seen him as yet Dad, lets see what he says"

When I go to see Dr. Ahmad he says what the rest say, that I need surgery but he is very pleasant and reassuring

"We do a laparoscopic removal. You will be in hospital for only two days and the scars are really very small and neat" he assures me.

I don't seem to be left with any choice in this matter. Taking the medicines I have been prescribed I undergo the necessary investigations pre surgery and the anesthetic check up, none of which is any discomfort to me for I am familiar with all this. I realize too, that I am being treated with a great deal of importance both by the doctors and the nurses and that makes me feel better.

I don't have any apprehension regarding the surgery for I have full faith in both my doctor and in modern medicine.

I do need to plan though and so I call Kiya

"What did the doctor say?" she demands cutting out the pleasantries.

"I need surgery, ASAP" Verbalizing it to her makes it seem more real somehow.

"Fix the date and tell me because I need to get organized too. I will be with you in hospital"

That is Kiya, my dearest friend. No "Should I be with you?" No "Do you need me?" but a loud and clear "I WILL be"

When I have a friend like this what do I need to be scared of?

Nothing.

After this conversation I cheerfully fix a date for surgery, all problems solved.

Later in the day I call Dad and tell him and he is practical too

"No need to worry, you will be fine, not a difficult surgery"

Sangeeta will look after Merlin and so most of my concerns are now covered. She may even keep him at her own house for a few days after the surgery so I can have some rest during the convalescence.

Mohit however reacts in a most undoctor like way. His line of thought is something like this

"Why is it necessary to have it out now? You may never have another attack of colic. The stones must have been there for years and may now stay silent. I think you can wait"

Is this a sign of worry or is it plain cussedness, I'm not sure. And then

"You must message me before you go in for surgery and immediately after it is over and you are conscious"

"I wont have my phone on me in the operation theater" I tell him, being practical,

"Then as soon as you have it" Mohit says again.

Possibly he is worried about me. I'm not sure how that makes me feel.

However with the consensus in favor of it I went in for surgery.

On the day of the surgery I meet Kiya at the hospital at 6 am and we giggle and laugh as we enter the room, which is ours for the next two days, for me as a patient and for her as my attendant. Kiya checks everything from the bed linen to the toiletries, appreciating the herbal soap and shampoo. You'd think we are here on a vacation.

My surgery went off smoothly, even easier than I had envisaged. I woke post operative, groggy and hungry and was given something to drink just 4 hours after the operation. Dozing fitfully as a result of the medication and the relief of being done with the surgery I lie in the hospital bed and watch Kiya play host.

Coming back to the room from the operation theatre I remember to send a message to Mohit on whatsapp

"All well, surgery done, will get back to you later"

"Thank God. That's a relief" is the reply I get.

From the afternoon to late evening I have a steady stream of visitors and the atmosphere is more festive and social. Dad is here and Kiya has seen to it that he gets some lunch and some rest. He is tired I think as I watch him but nothing would have kept him away so I didn't suggest it. Colleagues and friends all pay me a visit. Looking at all these people I realize that in so many ways India still holds on to its cultural values for whether it be a sad occasion or a happy one you will find lots of friends and family to rally around.

I appreciate all these people and their concern for me.

Late evening and my doctor comes to visit and I ask him
"I feel fine, do I really need to stay in hospital for two days?"
He smiles at me, commenting
"For a doctor you have been a good patient. If you feel fine tomorrow we will let you go"
I did feel fine and since I was so uncomplaining (I had nothing to complain about) I was discharged at twenty-four hours.

Actually the whole thing was a bit of an anticlimax.

Readying to head home, taking the medicines, which have been prescribed, to me, Kiya like a mother hen, fussing
"Now get plenty of rest. And since they have given you some time off take advantage of it. Don't be in a rush to get back to hospital"
We drive back home getting groceries on the way. These days it is multigrain bread with Kiya; brown bread is no longer good enough. She says
"I don't think it is really brown you know. I think they just put some color in it to make it look that way. We will get the multigrain"
Whatever.

Letting myself into the house I find the tiredness catching up with me leaving me feeling drained and wanting to rest.

I am fine, back home.

Still not willing to completely give words to my fears.

There is described in medicine or psychiatry as the case may be a state called as the 'Fugue state'. It means that the mind is capable of selectively blocking out certain times or events which are painful and traumatic to give peace or a kind of oblivion just to make it possible to go on. It is actually a major psychiatric disorder, which leads to amnesia, which is very selective, and maybe even a total change of identity. Whether it is true craziness is arguable.

I now sit in front of his photograph and try to confront those fears for I have at best a very blurry memory of that day. Yes I remember, but all I focus on is after, after. . .

And not on what happened then, and before.

Diven was diagnosed with carcinoma of the Larynx. It came like bolt from the blue for he was big and healthy and all that was wrong with him was that his voice was hoarse. With him being a smoker that was nothing to write home about, but with his voice turning gravelly and odd, we saw a doctor. He advised scans and there it was, a tiny growth sitting near his vocal cords.

Even at the time of his diagnosis the gravity of the situation truly eluded us for my faith in medicine convinced him too about the infallibility of medical treatment. Further investigation was worrying too for the scans showed some lesions in the lungs too.

We were offered surgery. But Diven was adamant saying
"If I have to live with a tube in my throat for life and no voice, I'd rather die"

The oncologist is a gem of a man, big, burly and gentle and Diven took a liking to him. We were told that he needed six weeks of radiation and that possible he would do well after that. And I believed, for I had no reason to do otherwise.

Taking him for radiation first thing in the morning everyday and then continuing on in my workday was not difficult and he treated it as he did most things, with humor. In the waiting area for the radiotherapy, he made friends with all the other patients, learning about their lives and then telling me at the end of the day. His voice, which was so soft at the onset of treatment, became stronger and with it grew our hope of his recovery.

In this time, I think both of us accepted that we might not see seventy together. But then, if we had only three more years we would make them count. And so both of us made that extra effort, I by cooking all his meals and doing all the little things he wanted me to do and he by being his usual self no matter what the effort cost him. As the treatment progressed I could sense he tired easily so I hired a driver to drive him back home after the treatment. That man is still with me.

All through the treatment Diven kept on saying
"Once this is over, we will go to Kashmir"
I questioned the doctor about it and he said there was no reason to not go.

He completed his radiation on a Thursday and I viewed that too as a positive sign for Thursday is the day I go to the temple.

And we started making plans for the future for we had been told that he need not see the doctor for three week after which he needed some bloods, scans and reevaluation.

Trying to bring normalcy to our life we were thankful and optimistic. And we kept on planning to go to Kashmir.

But that was now how it was destined to be

A week later, Diven giving me a cup of tea at 5.30 is says

"I don't feel too well"

"What's wrong?" I ask him, worrying and going up to him to touch him. Feels fine, warm and I take his pulse, feels good and strong about eighty beats a minute.

"I don't know" he says "A sense of discomfort here" touching his chest, right and left.

Not wanting to take any chances I tell him,

"We are going to hospital" and his reply

"I am not going like this, give me time for a shower"

So I took a quick shower too and got dressed.

Even at that point we both were largely unconcerned. As we walk to the door, Diven coughs and then

"Look" he shows me his handkerchief, which has blood on it. Bright red, fresh blood on it.

I am scared now and I tell him

"You wait here. I will get the car"

How long did that take, a few minutes and he is standing a few feet away from the main door. So I got the car and leaving it idling I enter the house. He is swaying slightly so I go to offer him support. He holds on to me and we walk the distance to the door, which is not even five feet. And suddenly I feel him slipping, sliding . . .

I made an attempt to hold him but he is heavy and I can't do it, so I let him slide down, holding him with my arms and as he does blood pours out of his mouth forming a big pool at the side. I lay him down and check. No breathing, no heart beat. I do know CPR and I do the steps as in a daze but I know.

He is gone.

Possibly a hemorrhage they said. The radiation must have pulled some vessel, which ruptured and bled massively.

Who knows?

Finally making myself think about it, letting go of the "What if's" and the "Maybe's" and accepting.

I look at Diven's photograph and say

"I have managed haven't I baby? Maybe not such a great job, but still,"

And I can see him smiling.

Yes I feel that wherever he is he would be happy if he could see me now.

Life is finally about living and maybe very similar to a game of cards at that. You don't get to choose the cards you are dealt but you play the best with the hand you get. The odds are sometimes stacked in your favor and sometimes not but play it to the best of your ability you must. That is the way of it.

And be happy with it. You can go on being sad, go on living in the past and let life go by or you can look ahead and be hopeful.

I am planning to look ahead.

I have so much to thank God for and I will continue to look at life this way. For undeniably there will be times when life is difficult, when the going is tough and the way uphill. But whoever said it was easy. But its worthwhile and I wonder

"Will we meet again? Somewhere, sometime, in another lifetime, maybe?"

Is it possible? All the stuff about afterlives and reincarnation. I don't know.

But I do know that in this lifetime I was fortunate enough to get a love that can last a lifetime and I will cherish that.

I lie down and sleep for a while. Sangeeta will be coming anytime and she is staying over with me for a few days. But the house is very quiet. I miss Merlin. The first thing I missed was his boisterous welcome and now when Sangeeta comes the first thing I say to her is

"Sangeeta, go and get Merlin back home"

"But Bhabhiji, he wont let you rest"

"I will manage," I tell her. "Just go and get him"

And that is the crux of the matter.

I will manage.

When Merlin comes back he is so jumpy and excited that I am convinced that my stitches or whatever they put there will come loose. But he listens when I tell him

"Behave yourself" he does just that settling on the floor beside the bed and dozing off.

I have slowly got used to being on my own and living with Merlin.

I have taken only four days off from work with the contingency that if I do not feel well enough I will extend my leave. But now I suddenly feel the fatigue of the last few days catching up with me and for the next two days I largely sleep and eat and do little else.

"Tweet, tweet"

This phone, it can be so disturbing at times. Picking it up I see the pictures that Mohit has sent me, pretty flowers,

"Get well soon"

Flowers, pictures

Nice. I am not sure what this relationship is all about but life doesn't offer any guarantees.

Why should the end be written before the story is? Maybe we can get along and then maybe we can't. Time will tell and maybe a bit of effort. Like watering my plants for they will die if I don't, giving it a chance without bias.

I go out to see my plants. The banana plant is just the same, ugly, plain and squat. Can't figure why I got persuaded into planting it. But then I look at the rose bush and going closer I see this little touch of pink practically hidden among the green.

A rosebud.

Moving closer I put out a fingertip and touch it gently, feeling the softness of the petals not yet bloomed. It is going to flower. I will have roses in my garden. I have faith now that whatever the future brings I will take it head on. For happiness comes from within you. Life can be tough, it can be hard, but there is no giving up on it.

My phone is ringing and I go inside to answer it. Looking at the screen I see 'Kiya mobile' flashing at me. She has just left so I wonder. I answer the phone
"Hi"
"Guess what?" Kiya sounds bubbly, excited and happy. She doesn't have to tell me, I know what is making her feel like this.

Kiya is going to be a grandmother. All her worry, all her stress forgotten as she gives me the news
"The baby is due in November. I can hardly believe it. Everything should go off well now"
"I'm sure it will," I tell her as I call off.

Ringing off, I feel a tug of nostalgia. We've come a long way, the two of us, from being silly schoolgirls with our hair in two braids tied in ribbons to now, getting older and hopefully wiser. All the ups and downs and we have had our shopping sprees followed by coffee and cakes. I hope we can go on doing it at seventy but now I also know that it may not happen and that each time we do it, we should prize it.

That is it, loving what we do now. Now is what matters, yesterday is gone and tomorrow no one has seen. Far too often we imagine the things we will enjoy, the goodies we store as the future and they may never come to be.

Like Vikrant's wedding for which I planned in such minute detail. My new saris with their newly tailored blouses for the occasion and I got unwell on the eve. I owe DM an apology for this one. I haven't been able to meet his daughter in law as I had wished to. But it's a small world for a few weeks later Dr. Misha comes in to train in our department in Pediatrics. And I was right; she does belong to a different part of India.

We don't really change do we?

I am content with my life.

There was a time, not so long ago, when I felt I would not be able to smile again or feel happy but I have managed to do it. Not that it has happened easily. I still miss Diven but now I hold him as my cherished memory. I do not think time can dim for me the tones and cadences of his voice or the memory of the curve of his smile. Nor can I ever get over the feeling that sometimes he watches me and laughs when I am being silly. And the fact that I believe even now that whenever . . . whenever the time comes for me to leave from this world he will be there to hold my hand so I am not scared.

And I still wear my ring.

Going back to work after a short break is a pleasure and I enjoy my work. I am still trying to cut down on the emergency calls but it doesn't seem to be on the cards as yet. I have to keep trying and sooner or later it will happen. More of the paper work and less of the hands on, well that too is something to work on.

In life one must chart out some basic goals, the same as when going grocery shopping. Doesn't make sense? Yes it does. When we make lists we actually write down goals and then we make an attempt to tick them off. And because they are written, they stay in our minds and we focus on them. Less room for procrastination. Makes them seem more real somehow.

For me now it is simple, I want to do the salsa, I want to be able to run, though I can't even jog, and I think I want to climb Mount Everest or at least I want to see it.

Dream often and don't be afraid to follow them. Even if you fail, you will have tried.

Mohit has got himself a regular hospital appointment, as in a nine to five job. I don't know whether to congratulate him for joining the herd or feeling bad that his splurge of independence has ended. He now has a longer and more demanding work schedule and is no longer able to do weekday lunches. He keeps me updated on his activities, but we haven't met in a while. As though my thinking of him has somehow conjured him up on the phone I get a

"Tweet. Tweet"

Whatsapp and that's Mohit. He has a long life I think to myself as I read the message

"We should meet sometime soon"

"Yes, we should"

Is it a coincidence for at this time I get a message again?

"Tweet, tweet"

Sara, I think looking at the phone. A while since she was in touch. I check the phone

"I may be coming to Delhi, Ma'am," her message reads

"That's good news" I message her in turn "All well?"

"Yes," and then "There is a man . . .I am giving life a chance again"

And with that I think to myself that possibly with her coming to Delhi I can solve some of my work issues too. Maybe she would like to work with us again and I can take her on as my associate or some such thing. There are possibilities.

Sometimes it is that simple.

I think to myself

"I too am doing the same thing. Giving life a chance, giving it a chance again"

Life does go on.